# Expressions From Lancashire

Edited by Mark Richardson

 Young**Writers**

First published in Great Britain in 2008 by:
Young Writers
Remus House
Coltsfoot Drive
Peterborough
PE2 9JX
Telephone: 01733 890066
Website: www.youngwriters.co.uk

SB ISBN 978-1 84431 448 5

# Foreword

Young Writers was established in 1991 and has been passionately devoted to the promotion of reading and writing in children and young adults ever since. The quest continues today. Young Writers remains as committed to the nurturing of poetic and literary talent as ever.

This year's Young Writers competition has proven as vibrant and dynamic as ever and we are delighted to present a showcase of the best poetry from across the UK and in some cases overseas. Each poem has been selected from a wealth of *Little Laureates* entries before ultimately being published in this, our sixteenth primary school poetry series.

Once again, we have been supremely impressed by the overall quality of the entries we have received. The imagination, energy and creativity which has gone into each young writer's entry made choosing the poems a challenging and often difficult but ultimately hugely rewarding task - the general high standard of the work submitted ensured this opportunity to bring their poetry to a larger appreciative audience.

We sincerely hope you are pleased with this final collection and that you will enjoy *Little Laureates Expressions From Lancashire* for many years to come.

# Contents

Zainab Oyekunle  (10)     18
Farqaan Mohammed  (9)     18
Homayra Mahmud  (10)     19
Mehvish Hussain  (10)     19
Simra Akram  (9)     20
Amaar Saleem  (9)     20
Rahmun Noor & Wahid Khan  (9)     21
Jebin Akhtar  (9)     21
Hamzah Zulfiqar  (9)     22
Mariam Ahmed  (9)     22
Hussain Rizvi  (8)     23
Fawwaz Ashraf  (8)     23
Umair Tahir  (9)     24
Iman Khalique  (8)     24
Minaam Ellahi  (9)     24
Humera Salamat  (8)     24
Kashif Ulhaq  (9)     25
Amenah Hussain  (8)     25
Hamza Rauf  (8)     25
Nasir Shakil  (8)     25
Adeefa Begum  (8)     26
Ambreen Khalid  (8)     26
Zaib Butt  (8)     26
Adiba Abbas  (8)     26
Aysha Begum  (8)     27
Fahim Ahmed  (8)     27
Amirah Zulfiqar  (8)     27
Mohammed Waqas  (8)     28
Iram Javed  (8)     28
Haaris Habib  (8)     29
Humera Ghafoor  (8)     29
Saghir Ali  (8)     30
Zenab Ali  (8)     30
Aliyah Ahmed  (8)     30
Shuaib Sajid  (8)     31

## Cockerham Parochial CE School
Emily Folta  (7)     31
Kate Ayrton  (7)     31
Brydie Bellis  (9)     32
Molly Ayrton  (9)     32

| | |
|---|---:|
| Austin McWade-Price  (7) | 32 |
| Jack Bellis  (10) | 33 |
| Emily Pye  (7) | 33 |
| Josh Thornber  (8) | 33 |
| Lewis Moss  (8) | 34 |
| Jacob Gould  (9) | 34 |
| Thomas Stuart  (7) | 34 |
| Abby Clapp  (8) | 35 |
| Robert Stuart  (10) | 35 |
| Annabel Simpson  (9) | 35 |
| Adam Ball  (10) | 36 |
| Jack Benn  (10) | 36 |
| India Dobby  (9) | 36 |
| Ross Hilton  (10) | 37 |
| Daniel Lamb  (9) | 37 |
| Alison Kellet  (9) | 37 |
| Sarah Jolleys  (10) | 38 |
| Eleanor Greenhalgh  (9) | 38 |
| Matthew Barton  (9) | 38 |
| Holly Nash  (11) | 39 |
| Jemma Benn  (9) | 39 |
| Joe Wrennall  (10) | 39 |

## Marus Bridge Primary School

| | |
|---|---:|
| Leah Duddle  (7) | 40 |
| Luca Di-Matteo  (7) | 40 |
| Matthew Edwards  (7) | 40 |
| Aidan Harrison  (7) | 41 |
| Megan Hession  (7) | 41 |
| Ewan Foster  (7) | 41 |
| Jack Hodgkiss  (7) | 42 |
| Ben Leach-Waterworth  (7) | 42 |
| Jacob Lloyd  (7) | 42 |
| Matthew Moore  (7) | 43 |
| Amy Lyon  (7) | 43 |
| Kieane McCullock  (7) | 43 |
| Joseph Schofield  (7) | 44 |
| Jack Talbot  (8) | 44 |
| Olivia Nealen  (7) | 44 |
| Amber Turner  (7) | 45 |
| Max Wilson  (7) | 45 |

| | |
|---|---|
| Cameron Barnes | 63 |
| Robbie Williams | 64 |
| Evan Rive | 64 |
| Elle Howard | 64 |
| Jake Denton | 65 |
| Leah Howard | 65 |
| Ryan Unsworth | 65 |
| Jessica Velloza  (8) | 66 |
| Olivia O'Neil  (8) | 66 |
| Ellie Walker  (8) | 67 |
| Jordan Quigley  (9) | 67 |
| Daniel Seddon  (9) | 68 |
| Lucy Worthington  (8) | 68 |
| Ryan Smith  (9) | 69 |
| Ben Williamson  (8) | 69 |
| Owen McGugan  (8) | 70 |
| Amos Wynn  (8) | 70 |
| Samantha Donachie  (9) | 71 |

**Mayfield Primary School**

| | |
|---|---|
| Cassie George | 71 |
| Rachel Birtles  (11) | 72 |
| Daniel Murray  (11) | 72 |
| Charlotte Rumley  (10) | 73 |
| Ashleigh Wilson  (10) | 73 |
| Joshua Freeman  (10) | 74 |
| Maisie Caffrey  (10) | 74 |
| Leah Csesznyak  (10) | 75 |
| Jemma Hales  (10) | 75 |
| Emma Wylie  (10) | 76 |
| Sam Ip  (10) | 76 |
| Lucy Eastaff  (10) | 77 |
| Dré McKay  (10) | 77 |
| Sarah Redman  (11) | 78 |
| Graeme Smith  (10) | 79 |
| Lewis Gledhill  (11) | 80 |
| Lauren Sampson  (11) | 80 |
| Madelaine Warham  (11) | 81 |
| Daniel Clarke  (10) | 81 |
| Ryan O'Sullivan  (10) | 82 |

Eden Hughlock  (11)                                   82
Taylor Clews  (11)                                    83


**Our Lady & St Paul's RC Primary School**
Rhian Hawthorn  (8)                                   83
Alexandra George  (8)                                 84
Connor Marsh  (8)                                     84
Shannon Flynn  (8)                                    85
Olivia Harman  (8)                                    85
Cameron Carty  (9)                                    86
Matthew Ashton  (9)                                   86
Luke Campbell  (9)                                    87
Genevieve Easingwood  (9)                             87
Emily McLaughlin Connell  (9)                         88
Cameron Burke  (9)                                    89
Mason Cleary  (9)                                     89
Danny Gregson  (9)                                    90
Joel Stott  (9)                                       90
Sam Burns  (9)                                        90
Toni Moores  (9)                                      91
Sarah Hughes  (9)                                     91
Darnell Shaw  (9)                                     91
James Heywood  (9)                                    92
Danielle Davis  (9)                                   92
Georgia Langley  (10)                                 92
Rebecca Hilton  (8)                                   93
Jordan Yusuf  (9)                                     93
Mark Butler  (9)                                      93
Ryan Cosgrove  (9)                                    94
Sam Gibson  (9)                                       94
Conor Sidebotham  (10)                                95
Kevin Brews  (9)                                      95
Oliver Gibson  (8)                                    96
Chloe Meade  (8)                                      96


**St Bernadette's RC Primary School, Lancaster**
Charlotte Hampsey  (9)                                97
Kezziah Copping  (9)                                  97
Charlie Seddon  (8)                                   98
Luke Stewart  (9)                                     98
Laura Holden  (8)                                     99

| | |
|---|---|
| Alfie McPhelim  (9) | 99 |
| Chloe Ashton  (9) | 100 |
| Morgan Townley  (8) | 100 |
| Amber Stewart  (9) | 100 |
| Salma Mahmoud  (9) | 101 |
| Toby Jackson  (10) | 101 |
| Eve Dodd  (8) | 101 |
| Hannah Usher  (8) | 102 |
| Mia Eccleston  (8) | 102 |
| Jamie Fowler  (8) | 103 |
| Adam Buyers  (8) | 103 |

## St Mary's RC School, Accrington

| | |
|---|---|
| Luke Terry | 103 |
| Kieran Bannan  (10) | 104 |
| Courtney Bellas (11) | 104 |
| Liesel Baron  (10) | 104 |
| Lewis Noone & Nicholas Widdop  (10) | 105 |
| Jack Taylor  (10) | 105 |
| Joseph Dwyer  (10) | 105 |
| Joshua Haworth  (11) | 106 |
| James Kelly  (10) | 106 |
| Dominic Jack Lord  (10) | 106 |
| Dominic Meadowcroft  (11) | 107 |
| Matthew Alan Lord  (10) | 107 |
| Daniel Robinson  (10) | 107 |
| Connor Taylor  (10) | 108 |
| Hannah Young  (10) | 108 |
| Tyler Chapman | 108 |
| Blaise Dewar  (10) | 109 |
| Jamie Gardner  (10) | 109 |
| Holly Moore  (10) | 109 |
| Ryan Ormerod  (10) | 110 |
| Shannon Norris  (10) | 110 |
| Sophie Remez | 110 |

## Sabden Primary School

| | |
|---|---|
| Harriet Lodge  (10) | 111 |
| Kyra Mellows  (9) | 112 |
| Elena Haythornthwaite  (9) | 113 |
| Eleanor White  (10) | 114 |

## Trinity & St Michael's CE School

# The Poems

# Water

Rain, rain, shiny as a crystal,
rain, rain, clear as a pool,
the rain annoys me
when it hits the window and goes . . .
*pitter-patter*
*splash*
*splash*
*drip*
*blip.*

Rain comes from a cloud
and rushes into the ground,
slithers into a cave,
jumps out and forms a stream
and turns into a river,
turns into water vapour
and then trickles back to the cloud.

Rain, rain, making their own song,
wild dancing along to the music of their own song.

**Muqaddas Azeem  (10)**
**Broadfield Community Primary School**


# Water Is The Best!

W ater drops from the sky
 A cross the ground going like a river
 T ime and time spreads around
 E very day and night
 R ushing to make a fountain.

**Hassan Gbajabiamila  (10)**
**Broadfield Community Primary School**

# Water, Water Everywhere

Water, water everywhere,
Water in the river,
It is very peaceful,
Water going *splish, splash.*

Water, water everywhere,
Water in the air,
Water inside the black clouds,
The water is ready to come out,
It makes a plop sound.

**Bilal Anwar  (11)**
**Broadfield Community Primary School**


# Water

Water, water everywhere,
Water in the tap,
Water in the shower,
Running down my back,
Every time I have a bath,
Water in my hose water,
Water up my nose,
Water like a diamond on my toes,
Water in a water gun,
Water to have a water fight,
Water gleams like a diamond in the sky.

**Shafique Mohammed  (10)**
**Broadfield Community Primary School**

# My Waterfall Poem

W aterfall, waterfall, you're so cold.
A waterfall, so peaceful and calm.
T he waterfall goes splish and splash.
E very day and night.
R ushing by the pond.
F ast and furiously
A nd people watch it as it goes by
L oudly
L ovely waterfall, you're the best.

**Rajan Abdulrahman  (10)**
**Broadfield Community Primary School**


# Waterfall

W ater, water in the air,
A cross the ocean,
T ickling as it rains,
E verywhere I go, splishing and sploshing,
R ains as I go,
F ighting in the sea,
A sking for water,
L aughing in the river,
L ying in the pool.

What do you feel about water?

**Selina Shahid  (10)**
**Broadfield Community Primary School**

# Water

Water, water everywhere . . .
Water across the street,
Water coming down from the air,
Water bubbling while I'm swimming,
Water in the dark clouds ready to rain,
Water dripping on my back
When I'm having a refreshing bath,
Water, water everywhere I go.

**Zeeshan Ali  (10)**
**Broadfield Community Primary School**


# Water

W ater splashing on my window,
A t a pace I can't believe,
T hunder crashing on the ground,
E normous puddles on the floor!
R ainbow, rainbow everywhere.

**Saqib Mahmood  (10)**
**Broadfield Community Primary School**


# Waterfall

W ater falling from the waterfall,
A iming from the sky, waiting to fall down,
T umbling from the clouds, waiting to fall down on the ground,
E vaporating from the ocean,
R ushing through the streams.

**Adnan Farooq  (10)**
**Broadfield Community Primary School**

# Water

W ater in the clouds,
A pproaching down, *pitter-patter,*
T apping on my window, *tip, tap,*
E arly in the morning,
R aining down everywhere.

**Shoaib Javed  (10)**
**Broadfield Community Primary School**

## Water

Water bashes,
Water thrashes,
Making loud bangs,
Water dripping,
Water tipping,
Water shining,
Water crying when the clouds are full,
Water, water we use,
Water, water reuse.

**Fatimah Masood  (10)**
**Broadfield Community Primary School**

# Water

Water, water everywhere,
Water, water in a puddle
Jumping in, jumping out
Having fun is what it's all about.

**Maria Khan  (10)**
**Broadfield Community Primary School**

# Waterfall

W ater, water everywhere for you and me,
A cross the sea, beneath the ocean,
T witching and twirling, tickling and curling,
E ngaging on the ground,
R elaxing in the clouds, as it doesn't make a peep of a sound,
F rozen in winter like a crystal that gleams,
A fter it rains a colourful rainbow comes out,
L aughing as we splash water in the swimming pool,
L ying in a cloud waiting to thrash down on the ground.

Do you like water?

**Assia Arkam (10)**
**Broadfield Community Primary School**


# Water Everywhere

Water is . . .

W hite.
A mazing.
T ough.
E arly.
R ain.

E verywhere for you and me.
V ery good.
E ven for us to live.
R unning down from the sky.
Y ummy to drink.
W onderful.
H eavy.
E ver so clean when I drink it.
R aining down
E verywhere.

**Jannat Hussain (11)**
**Broadfield Community Primary School**

# Waterfalls

W ater, water everywhere I go,
A cross the streams, making rivers,
T ickling me as it rains,
E verywhere I go water splishes and splashes,
R ivers are filling, streets are flooding.
F alling past the clouds,
A rgh! Water flooding in my house,
L aughing and swirling as it's falling
L et it chase, drop after drop,
S *plash, splish, splash, splish.*

**Zakia Khatoon (10)**
**Broadfield Community Primary School**


# Water For Life

*Splash, splash, splash!*

Water is cold.
Water is hot.
We drink water.
We swim in water.

*Splash, splash, splash!*

Water gives new life every day.
Water makes us healthy.
We use water to have a bath.
Water is beautiful.

*Splash, splash, splash!*

Water is tasty.
Water gives energy.
Animals use it to drink.
I love water.

*Splash, splash, splash!*

**Iqra Ali (10)**
**Broadfield Community Primary School**

# Water, Precious Water

Water is precious
Just like your child
Sometimes it may cause
A lot of trouble
But remember
Despite how much trouble
It may cause
Water is still very *precious!*

**Fatima Bibi  (11)**
**Broadfield Community Primary School**


# Water For Life

W ater is important for people
A nd it comes from rain.
T he water flows into small streams to make rivers.
E very river flows to the sea.
R ainwater will fall again.

**Mohammed Ali  (10)**
**Broadfield Community Primary School**


# Bubble Baths

*Splish, splash,* bubble baths,
It's really, really, really fun,
*Splish, splash*, bubble baths,
You can play in it all day long.
*Splish, splash*, bubble baths,
You can make drinks with it,
*Splish, splash*, bubble baths,
Let the fun begin again.

**Irum Anwar  (10)**
**Broadfield Community Primary School**

# Ocean

O n the ocean ships sail
C arrying gold and diamonds
E very wave goes high and low
A s the wind travels along
N ear the seashore the waves disappear.

**Mahdiyya Begum  (10)**
**Broadfield Community Primary School**

## Water

We need water to drink, to cook,
To wash our hands, have a bath with it,
Most of all it keeps you healthy,
Water is very important for life.
Plants and animals need water,
Water is shiny but has no colour.
Water in streams, water flows in rivers,
There is lots of water in the sea,
But lots and lots of water in the ocean.
Water will run from a high place to a lower place
And seek the lowest possible level.
Water is wet when it is a liquid,
It is hard when ice.

**Marwa Rauf  (10)**
**Broadfield Community Primary School**

# Water

Water is cool.
Sometimes water is hot.
Water is so beautiful and so clean.
If we drink water we don't like it.
Water is important!

**Khurram Mansoor  (10)**
**Broadfield Community Primary School**

## Water For Life

W ater is the best and water is fun
A nd it is the water you can drink forever
T hen the water keeps you healthy
E at and drink water is the best thing to do
R ivers and waterfalls are made of water

F orever and ever you will not live without it
O ceans have water in them
R umbling water in the river

L earning about water is fun
I ncredible waves come to get us
F ishes in the water
E verybody enjoys water.

**Aksa Saleem  (10)**
**Broadfield Community Primary School**

# Splash

*Splash, splash!*
Have a bath
Under the tap
Soap on your body
*Splash, splash!*
Here come the blue waves
It is going to take me away
*Splash, splash!*
Bubbles in my bath
I love bubbles in my bath
*Splash, splash, splash!*

**Aroosa Huassin  (10)**
**Broadfield Community Primary School**

# The Sea Or A Bubble . . .

Splishy splashy
The sea or a bubble
Sometimes causes a little bit of trouble.
Bubbles fly in the air,
The waves of the sea dance around with flair.
The edges of the sea are white
It is also bubbly and foamy in sight.
Bubbles work with water,
Mixed with Fairy,
People have a bath,
Just like my daughter.

**Zorah Parveen  (10)**
**Broadfield Community Primary School**

# I'm Drinking The Water

I'm drinking the water
The fresh water
I'm sipping the water
The clean water
I'm gulping the water
The cold water
I'm gurgling the water
The nice water
I'm sucking up the water
The tap water
I'm guzzling the water
The healthy water
*Water for life!*

**Nazia Farooque  (10)**
**Broadfield Community Primary School**

# King Henry VIII

Henry was a good king
But sometimes he could be bad
When he died he was fat
He ate meat, salt pies and sweet things
He had 6 wives.
His first one was Catherine of Aragon
She was not good for him
Second was Anne, she died
Third was Jane, she died
Fourth was Anne - divorced
Fifth was Catherine Howard, she was beheaded
Sixth was Catherine Parr - survived.

**Hamza Khan  (9)**
**Broadfield Community Primary School**


# Water For Life

Drinking the water
The fresh water
Swimming in the water
The clean water
Blowing bubbles
Big and small bubbles
Getting hit by water
By friends
Water is nice
And gives energy
So let's all say . . .
*Water for life!*

**Haris Hussain  (11)**
**Broadfield Community Primary School**

# Waterfall

W ater in the air,
A cross the stream and across the lake,
T witching and twirling wherever I go,
E ven when it's summer it still rains,
R eady to make a fountain of water,
F lowing past the cloud,
A fter a beautiful pretty rainbow,
L ying through the clouds,
L etting the rain past as it falls by.

**Anika Ahmad (10)**
**Broadfield Community Primary School**

# Mary

M ary
A peaceful
R eligious
Y oung

Q ueen
U ntil
E lizabeth
E xecuted her
N ever

O ffered
F ood

S pecial
C are to Tudor
O ver
T oo
S oon!

**Roukia Techache (9)**
**Broadfield Community Primary School**

# The Tudors

The Tudors wore big hats,
they looked like magicians.

Henry VIII was fat,
he wore clothes that were just the right size.

Earth houses with straw hats.

The Tudors, wore lots of layers of clothes,
they looked fat and old.

Under garments under their clothes
standing up straight and that's how it's done.

Old people everywhere,
some with sticks, some not tall.

Roses are red, violets are blue,
Tudors are stinky and so are you.
(If you're a Tudor!)

Swans, badgers, seals and otters,
they ate them all.

**Hamza Khan  (9)**
**Broadfield Community Primary School**

# Water

Water gives you strength
Lots of people don't have water
Thirsty bodies need water
Earth needs water
Rains around the world start floods
Floods mostly happen in Bangladesh
Obliteration everywhere
Reservoirs keep water clean
Lives are at risk if floods continue
Famine happens because everything dies.

**Zakir Sabir  (10)**
**Broadfield Community Primary School**

# A Song Of Henry VIII's Children

Jane left Henry alone with a son,
Who's been king for six years?
What is his name?
King Edward is his name.

King Edward VI died with suffering
When he was only fifteen.

After Edward's death,
His half-sister Mary became the queen,
She was unpopular with Protestants,
She married Philip of Spain.

She died early morning of 17th November 1558,
Was buried in Henry VIII's chapel,
Then came along Elizabeth.

Elizabeth was the last Tudor queen,
She came to the throne when she was 25,
With no marriage, died on 24th March 1603,
After 45 years on the throne.

**Maleeha Shah & Syeda Islam  (9)**
**Broadfield Community Primary School**


# Waterfalls

W aterfalls,
A lways moving,
T umbling on earth,
E legantly but,
R ushed,
F alling quicker than ever,
A nd now shimmers more than ever,
L eading towards freedom,
L ife's filled with water,
*S plish, splash, drip, drop.*

**Shabana Akhtar  (10)**
**Broadfield Community Primary School**

# Henry VIII

Henry VIII married six wives
He had some children
One boy, two girls
All together that makes three
The family of ten.

Henry VIII married six wives
The fifth one was Catherine Howard
Who was very naughty,
Meant to marry Henry VIII
But was looking for a man in the court.
She had lots of boyfriends
When Henry found out
He was very angry
And said to Catherine Howard,
'Consider your life but now your death is coming,
Because you should spend your life with me, handsome guy'
Now you're executed. *Slash!*

**Sidra Bashir  (9)**
**Broadfield Community Primary School**


# Water

Water is very tasty as a drink.
Water is as clear as diamonds.
Water is as shiny as a mirror.
Water is as cold as snow.
Water is important for animals.

**Usman Saeed  (10)**
**Broadfield Community Primary School**

# Henry's Six Wives

Catherine of Aragon
Was a Spanish princess
She had a long dress
But her hair was a mess.

Anne Boleyn was kind and helpful
She wore dresses made out of wool
She thought Henry's castle walls were dull.

Jane Seymour was his best wife
She had a son but he lost his life.

Then he saw a portrait of Anne of Cleves
And decided to marry in the autumn leaves.

Katherine Howard was 19 years old
Henry thought she was kind until he was told,
That she had a boyfriend and that was the end.

Catherine Parr looked after Henry until his death
And that was the end,
He couldn't take a breath.

**Sahil Javed  (10)**
**Broadfield Community Primary School**


# Tudor

T  he Tudors were rich, the Tudors were poor,
U  gly Henry with his fat belly,
D  rank too much wine,
O  tter, seals, badger, on his plate,
R  ichard the Third was his mate,
S  weet Henry the Eighth.

**Layla Ali  (9)**
**Broadfield Community Primary School**

# Waterfall

W ater, water everywhere, water everywhere I go
A cross the river, near the pond,
T winkles in the clouds, over the coast,
E ver so bright, ever so nice, sparkling in the light,
R aining on the ground like storms everywhere,
F alling over the land, across the sea, ocean, river and stream,
A fter it rained a colourful butterfly flies across the sky,
L eaving a glimmer of sparkles in the sky,
L oving and peaceful in a fluffy cloud.

**Zainab Oyekunle  (10)**
**Broadfield Community Primary School**


# The Tudors

T he men were fat, they wore a hat
H enry thought he could write the best stories
E veryone wore a wig

T he Tudors had a fight
U nder the best page of Henry's book he knew there
   was something to do
D ilemmas were made
O r if poor people wore red they got punished
R ed was for the rich
S trawberries were for the poor
   Henry rode the best horses.

**Farqaan Mohammed  (9)**
**Broadfield Community Primary School**

# Waves

W inding waves
A t the coast
T errible fear
E ating others
R emoving shells

F orgetting no one
O h how will people survive?
R emoving everyone from the bay

L eaving no one
I ncredible waves coming to get us
F earful crash
E njoying everything.

**Homayra Mahmud (10)**
**Broadfield Community Primary School**


# Tsunami

W inding sea
A t the bay
T errific heights
E lbowing people everywhere
R ight and left it goes

F rightful crash
O verlapping people on each other
R emoving the shells from the coast

L eaving people with joy or pain
I ncredible wherever it can reach
F earful bash
E njoy the games on the water.

**Mehvish Hussain (10)**
**Broadfield Community Primary School**

# History Of The Tudors

H ere comes the history
I s it what you think?
S ome think if might be Stuarts, maybe Victorians,
   it's gone in a wink
T udors, the wonderful Tudors, stinky people they were
O ne mistake and you're gone, say bye-bye to your head
R eally, go and check with them, uh oh, they're dead
Y ou really think you're tough? I dare you, go ahead

O nly you would be mad to go back then
F ried swan, grilled badger, what unusual meat they ate

T here and then Henry VIII, stroppy guy he was
H enry VIII married six wives, beheaded 2, I'd have used a gun
E veryone had two meals a day, 800 people they had to feed

T udors never took a bath, they must have stank the place out
U nderneath their clothes so many more layers were there
D resses, skirts, so many they wore on and on
O h how they quarrelled nobody knows, if I were there
   I'd be careful
R oses, War of the Roses, 17 battles, probably took 20 years
S tuarts, along came the Stuarts who ruled on and on.

**Simra Akram  (9)**
**Broadfield Community Primary School**


# Henry Tudor

Henry Tudor was fat.
Henry Tudor couldn't stand.
His leg was as skinny as a horse.

Old Henry Tudor executed his wives.
He didn't let them keep their lives.
The sight was awful when he beheaded Catherine Howard,
As their heads landed, smack on the floor.

**Amaar Saleem  (9)**
**Broadfield Community Primary School**

# Henry VIII

Henry VIII was so fat
No wonder he wasn't used like a mat,
He showed off too much,
He loved his lunch,
So now we call him big fat lump,
He ate so much, that made him trump.

Henry VIII was so rotten,
No wonder he had a big fat bottom.

He loved his sport, so we thought,
Henry VIII was buried in the floor,
Next to his wife Jane Seymour.

**Rahmun Noor & Wahid Khan  (9)**
**Broadfield Community Primary School**


# Henry The Eighth

H orrible Henry
E ager to win
N ever took rules
R oyalty was in his sin
Y orkists fought Lancastrians

T udors are bad
H ave they gone mad
E very one knows the Tudors

E ager to win
I  s Henry the Eighth
G etting along with his big mates
H ave you had enough?
T his is getting really tough
H enry the Eighth, the big fat man.

**Jebin Akhtar  (9)**
**Broadfield Community Primary School**

# Tudor Times

Henry VIII, a very clever man,
He had six wives.
Music was his passion
And hunting was his sport.

To be rich in Tudor times
And live in great lavish palaces.
To dine and gorge on,
Swans, badgers, deer and owls.

To be rich in Tudor times
And wear beautiful silks and brocades,
Embellished with jewels of every hue.
No need to wash our clothes;
We never had a bath,
Consequently we were extremely smelly!

**Hamzah Zulfiqar  (9)**
**Broadfield Community Primary School**


# Henry Tudor And His Six Wives

Henry Tudor,
Was a Lancastrian,
He had jewels,
He was a show off.

When he got married
To six wives
He did love them
But he wanted a son.

So when he was old
He could handle the kingdom.

**Mariam Ahmed  (9)**
**Broadfield Community Primary School**

# Chocolate Is . . .

Chocolate is . . .
Smooth as ice,
Brittle as glass,
Nice as leather.

I lick it,
It melts in my mouth,
I'm twirling my tongue in a circle,
It has a strong smell.

It's fantastic, it smells like hot chocolate,
Water comes out of my mouth,
It feels smooth, it looks white, it has lots of milk in.

It smells milky, it tastes yummy . . .
It melts in my mouth.

**Hussain Rizvi  (8)**
**Broadfield Community Primary School**


# Chocolate Is . . .

Chocolate is . . .
As smooth as leather,
Stiff as a solid,
Melting, molten chocolate.

As soft as wool,
Bitter brown chocolate,
Crunchy like cornflakes,
A delicious delight.

Chocolate is delicious.
It goes down my throat,
Sweet as honey,
A melting moment squared in shape.

**Fawwaz Ashraf  (8)**
**Broadfield Community Primary School**

# The Tudors

T udors were rich, Tudors were poor
H ouses were old with stained glass windows
E xecution if the King was cross with you

T udors wore lots of layers
U sually their meat was different from ours
D iets were different from ours
O ur meat is fresh and clean
R ich people ate a lot of meat like
S wans, owl and badger.

**Umair Tahir  (9)**
**Broadfield Community Primary School**


# Christmas - Haiku

As Christmas begins
We get presents on Christmas
Christmas is special.

**Iman Khalique  (8)**
**Broadfield Community Primary School**


# Winter - Haiku

Cold, icy, foggy.
Lovely snow on the ground.
Windy wet winter.

**Minaam Ellahi  (9)**
**Broadfield Community Primary School**


# Winter - Haiku

Ice makes a cold day.
Winter makes a foggy day.
Snow falls thick and fast.

**Humera Salamat  (8)**
**Broadfield Community Primary School**

# The Tudors

T errible Tudors with no computers
H orrible smells, no wells to get water from
E arly morning, time to get working.

T ight fright from Henry VIII
U gly Henry never watched telly
D irty bellies with some jelly
O ur belly smaller than Henry's
R ichie rich, ugly, fat Henry.
S shh.

**Kashif Ulhaq  (9)**
**Broadfield Community Primary School**


# Winter - Haiku

When the snow falls down
It covers most of the earth.
I like the white snow.

**Amenah Hussain  (8)**
**Broadfield Community Primary School**


# Snow - Haiku

Snow falls in winter.
It melts on the floor after
It's wet and muddy.

**Hamza Rauf  (8)**
**Broadfield Community Primary School**


# Christmas - Haiku

A cold time of year.
Christmas is good for people.
Most food is yummy.

**Nasir Shakil  (8)**
**Broadfield Community Primary School**

# Slippery Ground - Haiku

Snow turning to ice.
Slippery ground - watch your step.
Sun shines, the ice melts.

**Adeefa Begum  (8)**
**Broadfield Community Primary School**

# Ice - Haiku

The ice shining face
People listen to the ice
As you look at it.

**Ambreen Khalid  (8)**
**Broadfield Community Primary School**

# Melting - Haiku

Snow begins to melt.
A slippery and slushy ground.
Snow disappears.

**Zaib Butt  (8)**
**Broadfield Community Primary School**

# Snowflakes - Haiku

Snowflakes are shiny
They are wet, cold and white flakes.
Snowflakes look like stars.

**Adiba Abbas  (8)**
**Broadfield Community Primary School**

# Chocolate Is . . .

Chocolate is as smooth as paper,
Chocolate is brown in colour,
Chocolate has sugar in it,
Chocolate has a pattern,
Chocolate is hard,
Chocolate melts with heat.
It smells delicious and it's smooth.

**Aysha Begum  (8)**
**Broadfield Community Primary School**


# Chocolate Is . . .

Chocolate is . . .
As crunchy as cornflakes,
As runny as water,
As stiff as a solid,
It slowly melts into little pieces.

**Fahim Ahmed  (8)**
**Broadfield Community Primary School**


# Chocolate Is . . .

Chocolate is as smooth as silk,
It's a dream that I wanted like this.
As tempting as roller blades,
I want chocolate every day.

**Amirah Zulfiqar  (8)**
**Broadfield Community Primary School**

# Chocolate Is . . .

Chocolate is my dream,
When you look at it, it makes you beam.
It tastes like cream
And don't be mean with chocolate!

Chocolate tastes like melted milk in your mouth,
When you eat chocolate it makes you bite your tongue,
It makes you hungry,
It makes you want to eat one hundred.

It smells like mint Tic-Tacs,
It's like chocolate milkshake,
It tastes like Yazoo.
It is creamy in colour and tastes of . . . zzz.
I dream of a million people eating chocolate.

**Mohammed Waqas (8)**
**Broadfield Community Primary School**


# Chocolate Is . . .

Chocolate is as smooth as a smartboard,
As hard as ice,
Chocolate is as hard as a brick and as crunchy as toast.

Chocolate is as crispy as cornflakes
And sugary like sweets.
Chocolate is as delicious as an ice cream.

Chocolate is as small as a mouse,
As soft as bread.
Chocolate is as smooth as a metal door.

Chocolate is as soft as a pillow,
As brown as a conker
And as small as a rabbit.

Chocolate is as cold as an ice cube
And as smooth as a wooden table.

**Iram Javed (8)**
**Broadfield Community Primary School**

## Chocolate Mmmm

Chocolate is yummy, it makes me gobble it until I'm fat,
Mmm, I dream of a cocoa bean,
I like to eat chocolate more than meat.
Smooth, the flavour on your tongue like hot chocolate,
Yum, mmm, the taste swallowing down my tongue,
It's sweet and has lots of taste.
The explosion, yum-yum, chocolate.
When I look at it, it makes me hungry.
Mmm, the smell of it.
It tastes like the top of a chocolate biscuit,
It melts on my tongue.
Oh yes, the white yummy, melting chocolate
I just feel like eating it.
Yummy yum, it tastes so dreamy . . .

Oh no! The chocolate is *gone!*

**Haaris Habib  (8)**
**Broadfield Community Primary School**


## Chocolate Is . . .

Runny like a chocolate fountain,
Creamy like milk.
Yummy as Mr Willy Wonka's first chocolate bar.
White like snow,
Rough as a mountain top.

Chocolate melts slowly in your mouth.
It swirls round and around.
Suddenly the mint comes out and *mmmm,*
You swallow it and you still taste it.
It smells like hot chocolate,
It melts and twirls round your mouth,
It looks like Dairy Milk,
It tastes like Milky Bar.

**Humera Ghafoor  (8)**
**Broadfield Community Primary School**

# Chocolate Is . . .

Chocolate is . . .
As smooth as a baby's bottom,
It feels so delicious and I can leave it in my mouth
For a minute until it turns to liquid.

As strong as mint chocolate,
It's as sweet as honey, it melts in my mouth
And down it goes into my throat,
It looks like the colours of a tree.

**Saghir Ali  (8)**
**Broadfield Community Primary School**


# Untitled

Changing in my mouth, smooth.
It feels nice and smooth.
It tastes like yummy, smooth,
Milky and very, very tasty.
It smells like coffee and chilli.
It looks bonnie in its box.
It's a whitey milky colour.
Chocolate is yummy, tasty, delicious,
Nice, smooth and creamy.

**Zenab Ali  (8)**
**Broadfield Community Primary School**


# Chocolate Is . . .

Chocolate is my dream,
It makes me eat it,
It feels smooth on my tongue,
It looks delicious, it tastes nice,
It makes me feel dreamy.

**Aliyah Ahmed  (8)**
**Broadfield Community Primary School**

# Chocolate Is . . .

Chocolate is . . .
As smooth as creamy leather,
As brittle as glass
Melting for a moment on my tongue.

As soft as cotton,
Like creamy oil
Going slowly down my throat.

Chocolate is . . .
Creamy as caramel,
When I put chocolate in my mouth
It feels like I'm in Heaven.

**Shuaib Sajid  (8)**
**Broadfield Community Primary School**


# Love

Love is red like a bunch of roses.
It smells like perfume.
It sounds like a beautiful song.
It tastes like cherry.
It feels like a warm jumper.
It looks like a lady falling in love.
It reminds me of my sister falling in love with her boyfriend.

**Emily Folta  (7)**
**Cockerham Parochial CE School**


# Sunrise

Sunrise is yellow like a banana.
It sounds like a shooting star in the sky.
It reminds me of a hot country.
It tastes like a lime.
It looks like a shadow.
It smells like an orange.

**Kate Ayrton  (7)**
**Cockerham Parochial CE School**

# Fear

Fear's colour is dull like a foggy smoked sky.
Fear tastes like burning marshmallows melting in my mouth.
It also smells like dead flowers.
Fear feels like nerves when you hit your funny bone.
Fear reminds me of my first day at school.
Fear sounds like a hurricane whirling around in my head.
Fear looks like a devil.
Fear turns everything good to bad.

**Brydie Bellis  (9)**
Cockerham Parochial CE School

# Anger

Anger is red like a burning fire.
It tastes like hot chilli pepper.
It sounds like a thunderstorm coming from the sky.
It smells like smoke coming from the sky.
It reminds me of when I was naughty and my mum got mad.
It looks like a person with smoke coming out of his ears.
It feels like a hot pan when I've touched it
and burnt myself and I have said, *'Argh!'*

**Molly Ayrton  (9)**
Cockerham Parochial CE School

# Darkness

It is red, *tu-whit-tu-whoo*.
It tastes like a dead rabbit.
It looks like cheese.
It smells like lavender.
It feels like air.
It sounds like an owl.
It reminds me of someone dead.

**Austin McWade-Price  (7)**
Cockerham Parochial CE School

# Sadness

Sadness is stained red like the blood of a split heart.
It reminds me of the time I split open my face on a jagged rock.
It feels like a rabid wolverine planting its teeth into my throat.
It looks like a member of my family in pain.
It sounds like an evil laugh from a haunted mansion.
It tastes like venom from a black mamba snake.
It smells like a rotting rat carcass.

**Jack Bellis  (10)**
Cockerham Parochial CE School


# Fear

Fear is black like a TV switched off.
Fear looks like rubbish piled up.
Fear tastes like rotten raspberries.
Fear feels like the light being switched off and on all the time.
Fear sounds like Dad shouting in the front room.
Fear reminds me of Mum cleaning the toilet.
Fear smells of dogs' breath.

**Emily Pye  (7)**
Cockerham Parochial CE School


# Fun

Fun is yellow like a burning sun.
It sounds like hyenas.
It tastes like chips.
It reminds me of a football.
It smells like honey.
It looks like a bright lollipop.
It feels like a soft ball.

**Josh Thornber  (8)**
Cockerham Parochial CE School

# Hunger

Hunger is grey like a whale in the ocean.
Hunger sounds like thunder in the night sky.
Hunger looks like the stars are sweets.
Hunger reminds me of my food.
Hunger tastes of dark black clouds.
Hunger feels like someone is raiding the world.
Hunger smells like smoke crashing down from the sky.

**Lewis Moss  (8)**
**Cockerham Parochial CE School**

# Sunrise

Red is the colour of the sunrise.
It tastes like you are on fire in your mouth.
It smells like plain air.
It sounds like it is a beautiful place.
It feels like a hot football in the sky.
It reminds me of the beautiful Earth.
It is a beautiful sun.

**Jacob Gould  (9)**
**Cockerham Parochial CE School**

# Sadness

Sadness is the colour of red and blood.
Sadness reminds me of when someone is crying.
It feels like water is going down my chin.
It looks like someone crying when they've had a fight.
It sounds like a monkey screaming from the roof.
It tastes and smells like water.

**Thomas Stuart  (7)**
**Cockerham Parochial CE School**

# Hate

Hate is as dark as a blackbird's beak.
It feels like the touch of a dead tree.
Hate tastes like all the mean things in the world together.
Hate looks like a sad, dark, mean person
In a pitch-black pit reaching for the light.
It smells like horror floating in the air.
Hate sounds to me like a poor injured person calling for help.
Hate reminds me of all the sad things in the world
And of all the people fighting.

**Abby Clapp  (8)**
Cockerham Parochial CE School


# Fun

Fun is yellow like the red hot sun.
Fun sounds like a pack of laughing hyenas.
Fun tastes like somebody tickling you with a feather.
Fun reminds me of an exciting ride on a roller coaster.
Fun smells like the fresh air.
Fun feels like winning a trophy.
Fun looks like people laughing.

**Robert Stuart  (10)**
Cockerham Parochial CE School


# Hate

Hate is orange like fire burning.
It sounds like thunder and lightning.
It feels like an electric shock.
It tastes like hot chilli peppers in seriously spicy sauce.
It looks like a bull charging up and down.
It smells like smoke.
It reminds me of sadness and of all the poor people.

**Annabel Simpson  (9)**
Cockerham Parochial CE School

# Anger

Anger is red like a matador's cape.
It sounds like a steaming hot kettle catching the fire alarm.
It feels like blood boiling inside you.
It looks like a vampire with all its blood rushing down.
It tastes like a tomato sizzling in a pan.
It reminds me of my sister when she does not get her own way.

**Adam Ball  (10)**
Cockerham Parochial CE School


# Fear

Fear is black like a TV smashed up.
Fear smells like dead people.
Fear reminds me of when I snapped my football nets.
Fear tastes like burning sausages.
Fear feels like electric passing through your body.
Fear makes things bad.

**Jack Benn  (10)**
Cockerham Parochial CE School


# Darkness

Darkness is like a black hole.
It sounds like a horse stamping on the beach.
It tastes like chocolate cake.
It looks like the night sky.
It feels creepy and scary.
It smells like the ocean.
It reminds me of a dark sparkly night
with beautiful sparkling stars.

**India Dobby  (9)**
Cockerham Parochial CE School

# Darkness

Darkness is black like a gloomy bat fading into the night sky.
It sounds like an owl going *tu-whit tu-whoo.*
It tastes like black air flowing through the sky.
It looks like black with an owl's strange eyes.
It feels like the stars are sweets and the moon is cheese.
It smells like oak off a tree.
It reminds me of a power cut in the evening.

**Ross Hilton  (10)**
Cockerham Parochial CE School

# Laughter

Laughter is red like Man United thrashing Roma.
It tastes like strawberry milkshake.
It feels funny in my tummy.
It sounds like Nelson on The Simpsons.
It looks like people dancing on my tongue.
It reminds me of England beating Estonia.
It smells like chocolate.

**Daniel Lamb  (9)**
Cockerham Parochial CE School

# Hunger

Hunger is grey like a greasy grill.
It sounds like a tiger's empty stomach.
It looks like a giant plate with nothing on it.
It tastes like poor old soup.
It feels like a hug from Nana.
It smells like burnt chicken.
It reminds me of delicious food.

**Alison Kellet  (9)**
Cockerham Parochial CE School

# Fear

Fear is black like a TV, switched off.
It feels like someone is creeping towards you.
Fear tastes like spicy food on your tongue.
It looks like a damp old cellar.
Fear sounds like a crackling fire.
Fear smells like a rubbish dump.
Fear travels everywhere.
It reminds me of my dad when I've done something wrong.

**Sarah Jolleys (10)**
**Cockerham Parochial CE School**


# Love

Love is red like a beautiful heart.
Love looks like someone getting married.
Love smells like a rose.
Love tastes like a romantic dinner.
Love reminds me of the church bells.
Love sounds like a piano in the church.
Love feels like a new life.
Love makes me feel happy.
Love is for happy people.

**Eleanor Greenhalgh (9)**
**Cockerham Parochial CE School**


# Fear

Fear is dull like a horror film.
Fear tastes like an overcooked sausage.
Fear reminds me of chilli sauce.
It looks like a red-horned devil.
It feels like a brick falling on my head.
It sounds like a whistle in my ear.
It smells like oil mixed with fire.
It means someone is very, very overheated.

**Matthew Barton (9)**
**Cockerham Parochial CE School**

# Fun

Fun is yellow like the burning sun.
Fun sounds like a pack of laughing hyenas.
Fun tastes like somebody tickling me on the feet with a feather.
Fun reminds me of going on the big wheel and seeing
everything in sight.
Fun smells like the world spinning on its axis.
Fun feels like going on a roller coaster.
Fun looks like a big bright sunset.

**Holly Nash  (11)**
**Cockerham Parochial CE School**


# Sunrise

Sunrise is yellow like the border of my wall.
It feels like a star calling me into the distance.
It sounds like a hurricane hitting me on the heart.
It looks like a banana hanging from a tree.
It tastes like an apple crumble after tea.
It smells like a soothing cup of hot chocolate.
It reminds me of winter mornings when the sun is coming up.

**Jemma Benn  (9)**
**Cockerham Parochial CE School**


# Anger

Anger is red like an overcooked tomato.
Anger tastes like the spiciest curry.
Anger reminds me of the Devil with an evil smile.
Anger smells like Tipex overpowering my nose.
Anger looks like a large dark figure.
Anger feels like a dark abyss inside me.
Anger sounds like a hurricane twirling up inside me.

**Joe Wrennall  (10)**
**Cockerham Parochial CE School**

# Laughter

Laughter is red like some roses blowing in the wind
and a volcano falling to the ground.
It sounds like a volcano is collapsing.
It tastes like my tongue is going to drop off.
It smells like chocolate melting on my tongue.
It feels like my hands are really, really soft.
It reminds me of my cheerleading competition at the nationals.

**Leah Duddle (7)**
**Marus Bridge Primary School**


# Laughter

Laughter is yellow like good times.
It sounds like people enjoying themselves.
It tastes like chocolate ice cream.
It smells like melted toffee.
It feels like a nice hot summer.
It reminds me of thousands in money
and billions in gold and silver.

**Luca Di-Matteo (7)**
**Marus Bridge Primary School**


# Happiness

Happiness is orange like the sun in the sky.
It sounds like people laughing.
It tastes like chocolate ice cream.
It smells like strawberries.
It feels like a big shark biting my leg.
It reminds me of being on my trampoline.

**Matthew Edwards (7)**
**Marus Bridge Primary School**

# Laughter

Laughter is green like two aliens laughing.
It sounds like two laugh boxes laughing.
It tastes like warm hot caramel getting hotter.
It smells like a hot peppery Sunday dinner.
It feels like a comfy couch with warm bed covers on it.
It reminds me of lots of other times when I laughed so hard.

**Aidan Harrison  (7)**
**Marus Bridge Primary School**

# Laughter

Laughter is purple like lovely purple petals on a flower.
It sounds like a party at night at someone's house.
It tastes like drinking a cup of hot chocolate in the house.
It smells like I'm eating an enormous bar of chocolate.
It feels like a lovely cosy bed, staying up in bed laughing.
It reminds me of playing with my friends outside.

**Megan Hession  (7)**
**Marus Bridge Primary School**

# Fun

Fun is orange like a big juicy orange.
It tastes like tea.
It sounds like people shouting and laughing.
It smells like pizza with cheese and ham.
It feels like fizzy bubbles.
It reminds me of my friend at Darlington.

**Ewan Foster  (7)**
**Marus Bridge Primary School**

# Fun

Fun is blue like a football team called Wigan.
It sounds like a hot computer rumbling.
It tastes like very cold water running down your throat.
It smells like very thin white paper.
It feels like the printer printing loudly.
It reminds me of my dad's best friend who is called Kev.

**Jack Hodgkiss  (7)**
**Marus Bridge Primary School**


# Fun

Fun is yellow like on a fast roller coaster.
It sounds like enjoying yourself at the funpark.
It tastes like melting ice cream in your mouth.
It smells like chocolate melting in the air.
It feels like playing football in the park.
It reminds me of going in a funpark and going on rides.

**Ben Leach-Waterworth  (7)**
**Marus Bridge Primary School**


# Anger

Anger is red like a volcano.
It sounds like crying.
It tastes like horrid poisonous curry.
It smells like hot air.
It feels like a hard scaly dragon.
It reminds me of a volcano exploding with lava.

**Jacob Lloyd  (7)**
**Marus Bridge Primary School**

# Fear

Fear is pink like a flower.
It sounds like people watching really scary videos
while you're sitting downstairs watching very funny programmes.
It tastes like rotten beans sizzling like a mad buffalo.
It feels like you are swimming with the great white sharks.
It reminds me of my bad dreams which are really scary.

**Matthew Moore  (7)**
**Marus Bridge Primary School**

# Fear

Fear is grey like chimneys burning with fire.
It sounds like people screaming with fear.
It tastes like dry mud from a dry garden.
It smells like soup overcooking with steam in the oven.
It feels like hiding under the covers.
It reminds me of a really damp day.

**Amy Lyon  (7)**
**Marus Bridge Primary School**

# Fun

Fun is blue like the beach.
It sounds like a loud, noisy disco.
It tastes like melted chocolate.
It smells like chicken nuggets.
It feels like squashed, smooth grapes.
It reminds me of soft clouds floating by my eyes.

**Kieane McCullock  (7)**
**Marus Bridge Primary School**

# Fear

Fear is red like a volcano bursting on a house.
It sounds like people moaning because they have got lost
in the woods.
It tastes like spooky food coming alive and eating you.
It smells like smoke coming out of a chimney top.
It feels like a volcano erupting with lava.
It reminds me of lava pouring on some mountains that
people are living on.

**Joseph Schofield  (7)**
**Marus Bridge Primary School**


# Happiness

Happiness is orange like a beautiful yellow butterfly.
It sounds like orange birds singing beautifully.
It tastes like warm hot chocolate in my tummy.
It smells like yellow flowers in the garden.
It feels like a banana cracking in an egg.
It reminds me of a hard blue football in my muddy garden.

**Jack Talbot  (8)**
**Marus Bridge Primary School**


# Anger

Anger is black like a volcano erupting.
It sounds like I am going to pop.
It tastes like spicy chicken.
It smells like smoke coming from a volcano.
It feels like an angry shark.
It reminds me of an angry dog barking at a hissing cat.

**Olivia Nealen  (7)**
**Marus Bridge Primary School**

# Fun

Fun is bright pink like flowers.
It sounds like happy people laughing.
It tastes like tangy lemons.
It smells like lovely flowers in a bowl.
It feels like the bright sun.
It reminds me of playing in the paddling pool.

**Amber Turner  (7)**
**Marus Bridge Primary School**


# Happiness

Happiness is orange like the sun.
It sounds like barking.
It tastes like dog food.
It smells like sweets in a sweet shop.
It feels like hot chocolate with marshmallows on top.
It reminds me of my day.

**Max Wilson  (7)**
**Marus Bridge Primary School**


# Anger

Anger is red like a volcano exploding.
It sounds like people shouting loud.
It tastes like spicy curry.
It smells like fire spitting from a forest.
It reminds me of dogs barking very loudly.

**Katie Thomas  (7)**
**Marus Bridge Primary School**

# The Water Cycle

The grass is green, the clouds are grey,
Why oh why is it wet today?

There are streams between the high mountains of grass,
The streams run so fast!

The reservoir is so full,
If you look closely, you'll see a seagull.

Water gets through your home,
Pipes ship it to make your bath bubbles foam.

Your waste water goes to a waterworks to get cleaned,
As well you can get cleaned!

The water cycle ends finally,
At the sea!

**Solomon Glascott  (8)**
**Marus Bridge Primary School**


# The Water Cycle

The grass is green,
The clouds are grey,
Please don't come and rain today.
The sky is high,
The birds fly by.
The waterfalls splash,
Makes you dash.
A reservoir is big
And so is a pig.
The pipes take the water to your house,
It makes your bubble bath get more foam.
When you flush the water down the loo,
It makes it clean again, ready for you.
Finally all the water ends up in the sea.

**David Lockyer  (7)**
**Marus Bridge Primary School**

# The Water Cycle

The grass is green, the peat is brown,
The clouds are bright although the sun is light!

The sky is high and the birds will fly,
The streamlets will trickle, until they are dry.

The reservoir is deep,
Without a soul or a peep.

The pipes take the water to and fro,
When I jump in I go with the flow!

Finally the water ends in the sea,
So, see you again in a wee while!

**Kirsty Marshall  (9)**
**Marus Bridge Primary School**


# The Water Cycle

The grass is green, the clouds are grey,
Look at those raindrops heading your way!

The rivers run,
It looks like fun!

Reservoirs run for miles and miles,
All it will end up doing is falling on your work files!

Pipes travel to your home,
Drink half of it then make bath foam!

The sea is called a water den,
Soon the water cycle will start again!

**Elizabeth Yates  (8)**
**Marus Bridge Primary School**

# The Water Cycle

I can see the clouds are grey,
I wonder if it will rain today.

I can see the clouds coming down,
Just as fast as a brand new crown.

The hills are high,
The birds will fly.

The river will fall
And the fairies will call.

The pipes will give you water,
For your brand new bike.

The water will be cleaned up,
At the waterworks factory.

The rivers will run,
Back to the sea.

**Rachael Jones  (7)**
**Marus Bridge Primary School**


# The Water Cycle

The clouds are grey,
I wonder if it will rain today
When the fairy will call?
Water gets to your home
And gives you such a fright,
Pour it in your bubble bath after work
And it is full of foam!
The water ends in the sea
And the water cycle can start again and again.

**Rebecca Hampson  (7)**
**Marus Bridge Primary School**

# The Water Cycle

The grass is green and the clouds are grey,
I think it will rain today.

The water trickles down the stream,
Look at it gleam and beam.

Look at that lovely white waterfall,
As it trickles down that stony wall.

The dam stretches far,
You can't even get round it in a car.

The pipes send water to our homes,
You won't have to pay any loans.

Look at that watery den,
That is where the water cycle starts again.

**Taylor McDermott (9)**
**Marus Bridge Primary School**


# The Water Cycle

The grass is green, the clouds are grey,
Is it going to rain today?
The water splashes and the lightning flashes!

The reservoir is not far from my house,
Maybe you could find a woodlouse!

Water goes to my home,
Turn on the tap, hear it groan.

Finally the water cycle ends in a den,
Now it will start all over again.

**Marc Penn (8)**
**Marus Bridge Primary School**

# The Water Cycle

The grass is green,
The clouds are grey,
It is not raining, hip hip hooray!

The sky is high,
So the birds can fly.
Rivers are crashing,
Birds are flapping and twittering in the lovely sky!

The water is crashing,
Making rivers down below.
It will soon fill from above.

The reservoir goes so far,
Until it will not go along anymore.

To your house the pipes will go,
Make sure your bath doesn't overflow!

**Matthew Higson  (7)**
**Marus Bridge Primary School**


# The Water Cycle

The grass is green and the clouds are grey,
Is it going to rain today?

There is a stream at the bottom,
With a lot of blossom.

The reservoir goes so fast,
I think it is going to blast!

There are pipes with a lot of water,
Put it in your bubble bath and you will be in a motor.

The water is dirty when it is flushed,
But in the pipes it won't be rushed.

The rivers run to the sea,
The water cycle starts again at me.

**Aleesha Leonard  (7)**
**Marus Bridge Primary School**

# The Water Cycles

The grass is green, the peat is brown,
The clouds are bright, although the sun is light!

The sky is high, so the birds will fly,
The rivers will flow, unless it is dry.

The reservoir is high when I pass by,
The dam is big, as the water trickles by.

The pipes take water through to our home,
Put it in your bath and make it foam.

When the water overflows it will give you a fright,
As it travels through your pipes.

The water will flow down your pipe,
You flush it down the drain,
As you wash your hands again.

Then it all ends back in the sea,
When I return home to have a cup of tea!

**Jessica Ann  (8)**
**Marus Bridge Primary School**


# The Water Cycle

The grass is green and the clouds are grey,
Is it going to rain today?

The rain comes up above,
Falls on the hills and makes a huge river.

This is a reservoir that holds lots of water,
If you look closely you can see a brand new car!

The big pipes arrive at our houses
So we can have a nice bubble bath.

**Corey Morgan  (7)**
**Marus Bridge Primary School**

# The Water Cycle

The grass is green and the clouds are grey,
It doesn't seem to rain in May.

The water trickles down the stream,
Look at it gleam and beam.

The reservoir goes so far,
The only way around it is to go by car.

The pipes take the water to our homes,
Turn on the tap and here it comes.

Look at that water so clean,
To bad it's got to come out that beautiful scene.

**Jack Hardy (8)**
**Marus Bridge Primary School**


# The Water Cycle

The rocks are grey
The grass is green
The stream has a twinkly gleam.

The birds can fly
As the river passes by.

The pipes go round
Under the ground.

The shimmery sea
Makes a fun day for me.

**Kailey Tymon (7)**
**Marus Bridge Primary School**

# The Water Cycle

The grass is green and the clouds are grey,
Is it going to rain today?

The sky is high, the birds will fly,
Over the rivers, but some are dry!

Reservoirs are big and really far,
It will take ages to go round, even in a car!

Water goes through pipes,
You can drink it, you can drink it
Or you can send it back down again.

Finally the water cycle ends in the salty sea,
We need to start it all again!

**Nathan Hines  (8)**
**Marus Bridge Primary School**


# The Water Cycle

The grass is green and the clouds are grey,
Is it going to rain today?

The sky is high, the birds will fly,
Over the mountain high!

The reservoir goes so far,
Just like a very fast car!

The pipes take water to your home,
Turn the tap on, now it is going home!

Finally the water ends in the sea,
Then I see a reflection of me!

**Anna Wilkinson  (7)**
**Marus Bridge Primary School**

# The Water Cycle

The grass is green,
The clouds are grey,
Listen, can you hear the rain play?
Waterfall, waterfall, fly to the rivers nearby!

Reservoir, reservoir, you go so far,
Why oh why do you never say bye?

The pipes come to our homes,
So when we get home
We get a bath and make it really, really foam.

In the saltwater sea
The jellyfish and I say *yippee,*
To all the other creatures laying there
In that horrible salty sea!

**Amber Wilding  (8)**
**Marus Bridge Primary School**

# The Water Cycle

The grass is green, the clouds are grey
It's not raining, hip hip hooray!

The sky is high, the birds will fly,
Streams will run, it looks like sun.

The water is falling,
Down it looks, fun to watch it fall!

The water is flowing,
Through to your house,
You can bath in it and wash your hands!

The dirty water goes to the waterworks
And is cleaned.

Then finally ends at the ocean
And begins again!

**Jamie Talbot  (9)**
**Marus Bridge Primary School**

# The Water Cycle

The grass is green, the clouds are grey,
I thought it was going to be a sunny day today.

There are streams between the high mountains of grass,
The stream is rocky and it goes so fast!

The reservoir is so full,
If you look closer you'll see it will flood!

The water gets flushed down the toilet,
It goes to the waterworks,
They clean it then it goes back down again!

Finally the water cycle ends in the sea,
Some people call it a sea den
Then the water cycle starts all over again.

**Chantelle Milady (8)**
**Marus Bridge Primary School**


# The Water Cycle

There are many clouds in the sky,
That rise over the mountain high.

The sky is high, the birds will fly,
Over the rivers but some are dry.

Reservoirs are big and really far,
It will take ages to walk around and even in a car.

Can you hear the sound of the waterfall,
Because I can, it gurgles and burgles as you hear it call.

Finally the water cycle ends in the sea,
So then we start it all again.

**Leah Fort (8)**
**Marus Bridge Primary School**

# The Water Cycle

Now is the time to hide away
because I think the rain is coming today.

There are birds in the sky
and it's dry.

When the reservoir is full
and if you look very far,
you might be able to see the pier.

The pipes take the water to your home,
put the water in your bubble bath
and see it foam.

At the waterworks the water is cleaned
and purified but never dried.

After this the cycle ends,
at the twirly twisty salty sea
it might just start again, it just depends.

**James Ashcroft  (8)**
**Marus Bridge Primary School**


# Friendship

Friendship is purple like bright lavender.
It smells like sugary sweets in wrappers.
Friendship tastes like Dairy Milk melting in your mouth.
It sounds like birds singing in a tree.
Friendship feels like you do have a best friend.
It lives at the top of your soul.
Friendship never leaves you.

**Gabrielle White**
**Marus Bridge Primary School**

# My Sister

She looks like a silly, ugly, slavery dog.
Her hands are like a chubby elephant's hands.
Her face is like a round circle.
Her eyes are like a black dot in brown colour and white at the top.
Her clothes are like soft, nice pieces of material.
She moves like a snail.
She walks like a sloth.
She runs like an elephant.
She thinks she is quick.
I think she isn't.
She is very slow.

**Bryan Waite  (8)**
**Marus Bridge Primary School**


# My Sister

She looks like a star in my eye.
Her hands are like a newborn baby.
Her face is like a shining light.
Her eyes are like glittering stars.
Her clothes are my clothes.
She moves like an angel.
She walks like her mum.
She runs her normal speed.
She thinks I am a really nice lad
And always expects sweets.
I think she is beautiful.

**Cona Harris  (8)**
**Marus Bridge Primary School**

# Love

Love is the colour of bright red roses that blossom in the wind.
It smells like a flowery garden freshly planted.
Love tastes like Galaxy melting in your mouth.
It sounds like birds tweeting in the sun.
Love makes your body feel warm inside.
Love lives at the top of your heart.

**Rebecca Jones**
**Marus Bridge Primary School**


# War

War is black and grey like rain clouds in the night sky.
It smells like fresh guts coming from a soldier.
War is like blood coming from a dagger.
It sounds like a bomb blowing up a truck.
War feels like a bullet going through your head.
War lives at the bottom of your heart.

**Christopher Atherton**
**Marus Bridge Primary School**


# War

War is the colour of a pitch-black basement.
It smells like bullets being reloaded into a gun.
War tastes like blood coming from someone's head.
It sounds like bombs being exploded in front of your face.
War feels like a skull hitting your face.
It lives at the bottom of your soul.

**Matthew Holmes**
**Marus Bridge Primary School**

# My Brother

He looks like a tall lamp post and he is just the right size.
His hands are like Great Kahli because he has big hands.
His face looks like a wet lemon when he pulls a funny face.
He moves like a normal person.
He walks like a normal person.
He runs like a cheetah.
*He* thinks he is twenty-one.
I think he is the best brother in the world.

**Matthew Glover (8)**
**Marus Bridge Primary School**


# Friendship

Friendship is lavender pink, like a beautiful rose field.
It smells like gorgeous flowers in a daffodil field.
Friendship tastes like Galaxy melting in your mouth.
It sounds like children playing in a cornfield.
Friendship feels like a soft cute puppy.
Friendship lives in the middle of your heart.

**Kira Shaw**
**Marus Bridge Primary School**


# The Story Of A Line

A line can twirl
A line can swirl
A line can fiddle nicely
Sometimes it can hop like a mop
Or it can spin quietly!
Lines can jiggle, glide and grow or even curl
A line is amazing when it can win
And one thing it can't do
Is slide down the slide!

**Lauren Mawdsley (8)**
**Marus Bridge Primary School**

# War

War is the colour of dull black skies.
It smells of gases and chemicals.
War tastes like soggy mud going down your throat.
It sounds like a thousand grenades and ten bombs
                                    going off at the same time.
It feels like getting shot in the head.
War lives in a battlefield waiting to be found.

**Daniel Makin**
**Marus Bridge Primary School**


# Pain

Pain is the colour bright red like blood.
It smells like dead bodies.
It tastes like dried up brains that have been licked.
It sounds like people being tortured on a chair.
Pain feels like a dagger going up your spine.
Pain lives in the coldest part of your heart.

**Lewis Weekes**
**Marus Bridge Primary School**


# Happiness

Happiness is the colour of a red rose.
It smells like chocolates melting on a sunny day.
Happiness tastes like pink lavender in your house.
It sounds like sweet birds singing in your garden.
It feels like fluffy candyfloss moving in your bedroom.
Happiness lives everywhere in your body.

**Mariah Barker**
**Marus Bridge Primary School**

# War

War is black like a twirling tornado.
It smells like gases and chemicals.
War tastes like an enemy's heart.
It sounds like a machine gun shooting right next to you.
War feels like twenty grenades going off at the same time.
War lives at the bottom of your heart.

**Callum Connolly**
**Marus Bridge Primary School**


# Kindness

Kindness is a shade of every colour
It smells like sweet lavender
Kindness tastes like you're having an excellent shiny day
It sounds like you're talking to your bestest friend
Kindness is a good future
Kindness lives in a nice warm home
Kindness is at the top of your heart.

**Daniel Abbott**
**Marus Bridge Primary School**


# Happiness

Happiness is as blue as the sky.
It smells like ice cream in your mouth.
Happiness tastes like melted chocolate.
Happiness sounds like a lot of people playing.
It feels like a soft cloud.
Happiness lives at the top of your heart.

**Andrew Atkinson**
**Marus Bridge Primary School**

# Death

Death is the colour, grey like a storm cloud thundering above.
It smells like a rotting soldier lying there for weeks.
Death tastes like a dead man's heart being ripped out of his
                                      chest, blood pouring like a lake.
It sounds like a woman screeching in pain for *help!*
It feels like a knife being stuck through your stomach
                                            a thousand times.
Death lives in the coldest part of your heart.
Death is something you do not want to see.

**Joseph Connolly**
**Marus Bridge Primary School**


# Death

Death is the red of a dead man's chest.
It smells like a rotting man.
Death tastes like a man's heart ripped out
with blood running like a pouring river.
It sounds like people screaming, 'Help!'
Death feels like heavy rain on your window sill
when you're asleep, then you have a heart attack.
It lives at the bottom of your body.

**Bethany Wood**
**Marus Bridge Primary School**


# Love

Love is as red as roses in a blossoming field
It smells like a lovely perfume
Love tastes like candyfloss melting in your mouth
It sounds like singing birds up in a tree
Love feels like a soft teddy that's just been bought
Love lives at the middle of your heart.
I love you and I mean it!

**Paige James**
**Marus Bridge Primary School**

# Love

Love is the colour of a red and pink rose.
It smells like perfume going around the room.
Love tastes like a heart-shaped gingerbread man.
It sounds like two people listening to slow music and
watching the sun set.
Love feels like a very soft love heart pillow.
Love lives at the top of your life.

**Nicole Connor**
**Marus Bridge Primary School**

# War

War is the colour of angry dark red clouds.
It smells of fried blood that's just been cooked.
War tastes of boiled guts, about to be taken out of the oven.
It sounds like an atomic bomb that's just gone off into space.
War feels like a gunshot into your heart.
War lives at the bottom of the coldest place in your heart.

**Omid Azimy**
**Marus Bridge Primary School**

# Death

Death is the colour of dark grey clouds.
It smells like a rotten log.
Death tastes like blood in your mouth.
It sounds like a bullet being shot.
Death feels like being blasted with a gun.
Death lives at the end of your heart.

**Cameron Barnes**
**Marus Bridge Primary School**

# War

The war's colours are black, grey and dark smoke.
The war smells like blood on someone's body.
It tastes like bombs landing onto the hard ground.
War sounds like soldiers in pain and crying for help.
It feels like a tank has been fired.
War is in my heart.

**Robbie Williams**
**Marus Bridge Primary School**


# Death

Death is a black colour like misty steam clouds about to burst.
It smells like two-year-old blood and guts dried up.
It tastes like mud rubbing in your face.
It sounds like five atomic bombs going off.
It feels like you're getting shot in the head.
Death lives at the bottom of your heart.

**Evan Rive**
**Marus Bridge Primary School**


# Love

Love is the colour of bright roses freshly planted in the garden.
It smells like freshly made cakes in a bakery.
Love feels like Cadbury's chocolate melting in your mouth.
It tastes like Jelly Tots in your mouth all at once.
Love sounds like romantic music going on and on.
It lives at the top of your heart and will fade away never.

**Elle Howard**
**Marus Bridge Primary School**

# Destruction

Destruction is the colour of a fire which is red, yellow and orange.
It smells like a building ready to explode.
Destruction tastes like fire in your mouth.
It sounds like a rocket hitting a tank.
Destruction looks like a bomb exploding.
It feels like a rocket exploding on you.
Destruction lives in the middle of the coldest part
of your soul, heart and life.

**Jake Denton**
**Marus Bridge Primary School**

# Friendship

Friendship is like a loving teacher brightening up the day
with a blue sky.
Friendship smells like roses in a field, blossoming up the day.
Friendship tastes like a Cadbury's chocolate love heart.
It sounds like a bird's sweet song.
It feels like someone hugging you.
Friendship lives in the very middle of your heart.
Friendship is so cute.

**Leah Howard**
**Marus Bridge Primary School**

# War

War is the colour of dark red like blood.
It smells like dead bodies burning.
War tastes like infesting maggots.
It sounds like a rifle going through your brain.
War feels like squashy lungs about to explode.
War lives at the bottom of a deep dark pit.

**Ryan Unsworth**
**Marus Bridge Primary School**

# My Sister

My sister
She looks like a pencil, small and thin
Her hands are like a monkey's, furry and fat
Her face is like a white face with about a hundred dots on
Her eyes are like a blue dot in the middle of her eyes
Her clothes are very scruffy and weird
She moves like a cat
She walks like a dog
She runs like a chimpanzee
She thinks she is very funny
I think she is very weird and not funny.

**Jessica Velloza (8)**
**Marus Bridge Primary School**


# My Brother

My brother
He looks like his mum
His hands are as white as snow
His face is like a beautiful flower
His eyes are like the blue sky
His clothes are always clean and sparkling
He moves like a squirrel, very fast
He walks like a tortoise, really slow
He runs like a rabbit, very quick
He thinks he's an elephant that's very clever
I think he's kind and beautiful.

**Olivia O'Neil (8)**
**Marus Bridge Primary School**

## My Sister

She looks like a rock star.
Her hands are like a normal person's hands.
Her face is like mine.
Her eyes are like big brown pebbles.
Her clothes are gorgeous and shiny.
She moves like a pop star.
She walks like a posh person.
She runs like my dad.
She thinks she doesn't look nice.
I think she looks nicer than me.

**Ellie Walker  (8)**
**Marus Bridge Primary School**


## My Sister

She looks like a princess
Her hands are thin and small
Her face is like a pancake
Her eyes are like circles
Her clothes are trendy
She moves like a fashion girl
She walks like a lion
She runs like a cheetah
She thinks she's the boss
I think she's a little monkey.

**Jordan Quigley  (9)**
**Marus Bridge Primary School**

# My Sister

She looks like a chimpanzee.
Her hands are furry and slimy.
Her face is like my dog's, funny and cute.
Her eyes are like a witch's eyes.
Her clothes are beautiful and fashionable.
She moves like a lion in a forest.
She walks like a normal human.
She runs like a monkey in a tree.
She thinks she is a pretty girl and a good singer.
I think she's not.

**Daniel Seddon  (9)**
**Marus Bridge Primary School**


# My Brother

He looks like a lion, small and fat.
His hands are like stumps and big bananas.
His face is like an apple, round and large.
His eyes are like two lost dots in the sky.
His clothes are all Wigan tracksuits.
He moves like a girl running from a dog.
He walks like he's got two left feet.
He runs like the wind.
He thinks he is clever and good and brainy.
I think he is joking.

**Lucy Worthington  (8)**
**Marus Bridge Primary School**

## My Brother

He looks like a monkey and is very cheeky.
His hands are like a cat with hairy paws.
His face is like a round one but funny shaped.
His eyes are like two rugby balls with dots on them.
His clothes are like a caveman, ripped and very torn.
He moves like a fat elephant.
He runs like wind running through grass.
He thinks he is very clever.
I think not!

**Ryan Smith  (9)**
**Marus Bridge Primary School**


## My Sister

She looks like a little angel
Her hands are like a big peach dot with fingers
Her face is like a big cherry
Her eyes are like a kiwi fruit with a black dot in the middle
Her clothes are like some wedding dresses
She moves like a tiger
She walks like the queen
She runs like a Formula 1 racing car
She thinks she is beautiful
I think she is beautiful too!

**Ben Williamson  (8)**
**Marus Bridge Primary School**

## My Sister

She looks like a tiger
Her hands are like a bunch of bananas
Her face is like hairy coconut
Her eyes are like two bright lights
Her clothes are cute
She moves like lightning
She walks like a snail
She runs like a dog
She thinks she is cool
I think she is the best sister in the world.

**Owen McGugan (8)**
**Marus Bridge Primary School**


## My Brother

He looks like a chimpanzee
His hands are like feeling a soft sheet
His face is like a smooth pebble
His eyes are like the shining moonlight
His clothes are like an adventurer's
He moves like a robot
He walks like a snail
He runs like a cheetah
He thinks he's smarter than me
I think he's annoying.

**Amos Wynn (8)**
**Marus Bridge Primary School**

# My Sister

She looks like a princess
Her hands are like a spider's webbed hands
Her face is like a round pancake
Her eyes are like twinkly stars
Her clothes are like pop star clothes
She moves like a normal person
She walks like a rabbit
She runs like a monkey
She thinks she is cool
I think she's not.

**Samantha Donachie  (9)**
**Marus Bridge Primary School**

# Boom Town

*(Inspired by 'Macbeth')*

Round about the cauldron go,
Then throw in an old folk's toe,
Next up is some fat fingers,
Throw in a foot that lingers.
Stir it easy, nice and good,
Then put more in, like we should,
'Double, double, toil and trouble,
Fire burn and cauldron bubble'.

To blow up someone you hate
Just pretend you are their mate,
Sneak something in their pocket,
It's a bomb in a locket.
Wait until the time has come
Then you'll know they're not a chum.

**Cassie George**
**Mayfield Primary School**

# To Make Annoying Bill Die

*(Inspired by 'Macbeth')*

Round about the cauldron go,
Then put in some flies that grow.
Make a spell that's light and right,
Make sure someone's had a fright.
Then put in a juicy rat,
Nothing's good without some bats.
'Double, double, toil and trouble,
Fire burn and cauldron bubble'.

Then put in a tail of pig,
Add in some manky old wigs.
Then the time comes for wolf brain,
Mix it up and add a cane.
Flowers so deadly that kill,
Then kill young, horrible Bill.
'Double, double, toil and trouble,
Fire burn and cauldron bubble'.

**Rachel Birtles (11)**
**Mayfield Primary School**


# Witches Poem

*(Inspired by 'Macbeth')*

Round about the cauldron go
Through a jar of golden snow
Then throw in a dirty mole.

From the spirits get their soul
Then put in a greasy toe
And put in a muddy doe.

'Double, double toil and trouble
Fire burn and cauldron bubble'.
Ha ha ha ha ha!

**Daniel Murray (11)**
**Mayfield Primary School**

# The Macbeth Rap

*Inspired by 'Macbeth'*

Macbeth and Banquo were walkin' down da street,
When three ugly witches they did meet,
They had crippled fingers and shrivelled toes,
And one of da three ad a massive nose.

The witches predicted Macbeth would be king,
But Banquo's son will 'ave all da bling,
It's like they'd planted a seed in his head,
One night he stabbed the king, he was dead,
He's feeling guilty, what should he do?
I think he's evil, how about you?
Macbeth is now da king of da land,
He went to the witches to see what they had planned.

The witches said beware of Macduff,
But Macbeth thought it was just a bluff,
Macbeth didn't know what was going on,
People fought against him - not just one,
Millions of people wanted him dead,
Macduff did the deed and there he bled.

**Charlotte Rumley  (10)**
**Mayfield Primary School**


# Witches Poem

*(Inspired by 'Macbeth')*

Round about the cauldron go,
Eye of baboon in we throw.

Now throw in a nose of hog,
Then throw in a great big frog.

Now let's throw in a dog's leg,
'Yes!' one of the witches said.

'Double, double, toil and trouble,
Fire burn and cauldron bubble'.

**Ashleigh Wilson  (10)**
**Mayfield Primary School**

# The Witches Poem

*(Inspired by 'Macbeth')*

*A spell to have easy work at school.*

Round about the cauldron go,
A wing of bat in we throw.
Leg of cow, blood of man,
Beer from a drunk old man.
We throw in the cauldron now,
The bleeding heart of a cow.
'Double, double, toil and trouble,
Fire burn and cauldron bubble'.

Fillet of a fenny snake,
In the cauldron boil and bake.
You punish us with hard work,
Throw in my dad's credit card.
Throw in the answer booklet,
Now make sheets for all the kids.
'Double, double, toil and trouble,
Fire burn and cauldron bubble'.

**Joshua Freeman  (10)**
**Mayfield Primary School**


# Witches Poem

*(Inspired by 'Macbeth')*

Round about the cauldron go,
In we throw a giant toe.

Now we throw in guts of frog,
Then we throw in head of dog.

Then we want to throw in me,
Now for our teacher, Miss C.

'Double, double, toil and trouble,
Fire burn and cauldron bubble'.

**Maisie Caffrey  (10)**
**Mayfield Primary School**

# The Car Stealer

*(Inspired by 'Macbeth')*

Round about the cauldron go
Next throw in a blind cat's toe
Then a mussel from the sea
And then some blood just from me
Next to the sky we do go,
Then add a little essence of crow
Round to the new moon of gloom.

Fillet of a fenny snake
This is what I shall now bake
Eye of newt and toe of dog
Slippery mud from the bog
Now I cast this horrid spell
To get all cars in one well
'Double, double toil and trouble
Fire burn and cauldron bubble'.

**Leah Csesznyak (10)**
**Mayfield Primary School**


# Witches Poem

*(Inspired by 'Macbeth')*

Round about the cauldron go,
Eye of baboon in we throw.

Now throw in a nose of hog,
Then throw in a great big frog.

Stir it, mix it, nice and slow,
Let it bubble, let it glow.

'Double, double, toil and trouble,
Fire burn and cauldron bubble'.

**Jemma Hales (10)**
**Mayfield Primary School**

# A Rap To Tell The Story About Macbeth

*(Inspired by 'Macbeth')*

Macbeth went walkin' in da middle of da night
When he saw three old hags that gave him a fright.
The witches were ugly, evil as well
They got angry and cast a spell.

Macbeth woke up in da middle of da night
When he saw King Duncan, in his sight.
He got a dagger and killed the king
Then Macbeth took all the bling.
Macbeth couldn't believe what he had done,
Lady Macbeth thought they had won.

King Duncan's sons created a war
Against Macbeth the Thane of Caudor.
Macduff the knight killed Macbeth
And that is how he met his death.

**Emma Wylie  (10)**
**Mayfield Primary School**


# Witches Poem

*(Inspired by 'Macbeth')*

Round about the cauldron go
Put in a manky rat's toe
Then put in a tail of a cat
Then chuck in a bleeding rat
Then pluck an old witch's nose
Along with a garden hose
'Double, double, toil and trouble
Fire burn and cauldron bubble'.

**Sam Ip  (10)**
**Mayfield Primary School**

# The Spell To Make Annoying People Fat
*(Inspired by 'Macbeth')*

Round about the cauldron go,
Add a sticky, muddy row.
Then an eyeball from a cat,
Make the drinker very fat.
Add a jar of human bones,
Stop the wailing, stop the moans.
'Double, double, toil and trouble,
Fire burn and cauldron bubble'.

Fillet of a fenny snake,
Lovely rats without a crate.
Add in a rocker's wallet,
Full of sick, full of vomit.
Snakes' venom and foxes' goo,
Rabbits' ears and mouse's poo.
'Double, double, toil and trouble,
Fire burn and cauldron bubble'.

**Lucy Eastaff  (10)**
**Mayfield Primary School**

# The Witches Poem
*(Inspired by 'Macbeth')*

Round about the cauldron go,
Throw in the rotten dead toe.
Then throw in a monkey's eye,
Whoever drinks this will die.
Throw in a dead rotten rat,
Which has lots of fattening fat.
'Double, double, toil and trouble,
Fire burn and cauldron bubble'.

**Dré McKay  (10)**
**Mayfield Primary School**

# A Spell To Make Troubles Disappear

*(Inspired by 'Macbeth')*

Round about the cauldron go
Throw in some red eyes that glow
Mix it in until it's sweet
Don't forget the gruesome feet
Let it rest and hear it say
Make my troubles go away
'Double, double, toil and trouble
Fire burn and cauldron bubble'.

Fillet of a fenny snake
Woman's brain and bones that break
Boy's eyeballs and Granny's toe
Then mix it in, nice and slow
Lion's tooth and black bat's wing
Dark moonlight and princess's ring
'Double, double, toil and trouble
Fire burn and cauldron bubble'.

**Sarah Redman (11)**
**Mayfield Primary School**

# A Spell To Get Rid Of My Brother

*(Inspired by 'Macbeth')*

Round about the cauldron go,
A wing of bat in we throw.
Make my brother go away,
When he's gone we'll shout hooray.
Let's throw in a rabbit's ear,
With an antler from a deer.

'Double, double, toil and trouble,
Fire burn and cauldron bubble'.

Fillet of a fenny snake,
Then put in my rat poo bake.
Put in then a pig heart pie,
That will make him scream and cry.
Cobra's tongue and bear's claw,
A spider's sting, now I'm sure.

'Double, double, toil and trouble,
Fire burn and cauldron bubble'.

**Graeme Smith  (10)**
**Mayfield Primary School**

# The Spell To Take Spirits

*(Inspired by 'Macbeth')*

Round about the cauldron go,
Let's throw in a manky toe.
Heart of dragon, tongue of frog,
Let us make this horrid grog.
Now let us get more sea salt,
Now let us see that they halt.

'Double, double, toil and trouble,
Fire burn and cauldron bubble'.

Fillet of a fenny snake,
Tail of mouse, let us now take.
A bird's wing, horribly new,
Throw that in, let's make them spew!
A broken sword drenched in blood,
Let us get their soul for good!

'Double, double toil and trouble,
Fire burn and cauldron bubble'.

**Lewis Gledhill  (11)**
**Mayfield Primary School**

# Witches Poem

*(Inspired by 'Macbeth')*

Round about the cauldron go,
Then chuck in a slimy toe.
Then throw in an old man's hand,
Cast a spell with magic sand.
In go frogs and old dead dogs,
Mix it up with a thick log.
'Double, double, toil and trouble,
Fire burn and cauldron bubble'.

**Lauren Sampson  (11)**
**Mayfield Primary School**

# A Rap To Tell The Story Of Macbeth

*(Inspired by 'Macbeth')*

Macbeth and Banquo went walkin' in da night,
Three witches appeared and gave dem a fright.
Da witches looked like men but were actually wimen,
Their fingers looked light, they had just been swimmin'.
Da witches told Macbeth he was gonna be loyal,
As good as Prince Charmin' or even as royal.

Mac invited King Duncan to his castle,
But it ended up one big hassle.
In da middle of da night he got his sword,
Killed King Duncan, being king was his reward,
People were suspicious about Macbeth,
So they planned for his big death.
Duncan's son created a war,
To fight against Macbeth, that's what it's for.
In de end Macbeth dies,
Down in Hell his spirit lies.

**Madelaine Warham  (11)**
**Mayfield Primary School**


# Witches Poem

*(Inspired by 'Macbeth')*

Round about the cauldron go.
In it goes a minging toe.
From your nose some sticky snot,
Stir and stir around the pot.
Stir it nice and very hot,
Next add in some pretty dots.
'Double, double, toil and trouble,
Fire burn and cauldron bubble'.

**Daniel Clarke  (10)**
**Mayfield Primary School**

# A Rap To Tell The Story Of Macbeth

*(Inspired by 'Macbeth')*

Macbeth went walkin' in the night.
When he saw three witches that gave him a fright.
The witches are ugly, evil as well,
They got very angry and cast a spell.

He woke up in the middle of the night,
When he saw King Duncan in his sight.
He grabbed a dagger and killed the King,
Then Macbeth took all the bling.

King Duncan's sons created a war
Against Macbeth, the thane of Cawdor.
Macduff the knight killed Macbeth
And that is how he met his death.

**Ryan O'Sullivan  (10)**
**Mayfield Primary School**


# Macbeth Witches Poem

*(Inspired by 'Macbeth')*

Round about the cauldron go,
Let's throw in a manky toe.
Heart of dragon, tongue of frog,
Let us make this horrid grog.
Put this spell on my brother,
Now let me see his mother.
'Double, double, toil and trouble,
Fire burn and cauldron bubble'.

Fillet of a fenny snake,
Now let's go and bake that cake.
Wool of sheep from his small feet,
Don't forget to add some meat.
Mix it up with a big spoon,
To make this spell full of doom.
'Double, double, toil and trouble,
Fire burn and cauldron bubble'.

**Eden Hughlock  (11)**
**Mayfield Primary School**

# A Spell To Get Rid Of Homework

*(Inspired by 'Macbeth')*

Round about the cauldron go,
Toe of rhino, eye of Moe!
Lob it all in, stir it round,
Then throw in a poisoned hound.
Wing of raven, nose of cat,
Then throw in a mouldy rat.
'Double, double, toil and trouble,
Fire burn and cauldron bubble'.

Fillet of a fenny snake,
Stir it with a strong rake.
Dragon's nails, he's called Peter,
Leg of sheep, fang of cheetah.
Blood and gut, heart and kidney,
Peter's dad, he's called Sidney.
'Double, double, toil and trouble,
Fire burn and cauldron bubble'.

**Taylor Clews  (11)**
**Mayfield Primary School**

# Nobody Knows

I have an alien in my wardrobe
and he can be a little mean,
he has big ears and his skin is green.
He is furry and is always early
for meetings about being clean.
He took me to Mars to meet his mum and dad
but I didn't like it so we went home,
shopping for a new handbag.
His favourite colour is purple
because it matches all his things.
He has big claws and he's six foot tall.
He has a blue nose
and likes to show off his diamond toes.

**Rhian Hawthorn  (8)**
**Our Lady & St Paul's RC Primary School**

# The Alien From Planet X

I have an alien, she lives in the sea
and her name is Diamond.
She has her breakfast on the sunbed at the beach
and her drink always leaks.
Now I am going to tell you all about her.
She has seven tentacles,
she loves Valentine's cards
and she always brings me flowers.
She's green, black, blue, red, pink
and she's really cute.
She loves doing the things I do,
she always remembers everything
and she loves rings.

**Alexandra George  (8)**
**Our Lady & St Paul's RC Primary School**


# About My Alien

My alien lives in an ice cream van.
My alien loves ice cream.
He loves to bang his head.
My alien likes me.
He drives to the beach and plays with the sand.
All night long he splashes in the sea.
He catches fish and keeps them as pets.
His purple hair looks weird and wet.

**Connor Marsh  (8)**
**Our Lady & St Paul's RC Primary School**

# My Alien From The Milky Way

I have an alien under my settee,
She likes to eat her tea with me.
She sleeps on my bedroom floor,
She wakes me up by knocking on my bedroom door.
My alien is called Sky
And her favourite food is pie.
Sky took me to the Milky Way one day
To see her mum and dad, Bob and May.
When we got back,
I had a big sack,
I put the sack down
And fell down on the ground.
My alien Sky has brown eyes,
Has a sausage for a nose.
She has black teeth and big fat feet.

**Shannon Flynn  (8)**
**Our Lady & St Paul's RC Primary School**

# My Best Friend Alien Max

I have an alien in my mum's shed
And he eats his breakfast in my brother's bed,
His eyes are purple and his fingers are pink,
He's friendly and nice
And he has sweets when I go to school,
After school he acts really cool,
When I go to bed he acts the same again,
His nose is white and his legs are black,
He has a belly that looks like jelly
And his name is Max.

**Olivia Harman  (8)**
**Our Lady & St Paul's RC Primary School**

# The Alien I Think I Saw

He may be big,
He may be small,
He can live anywhere at all,
I thought I saw him near my football.

He has six or seven eyes,
He's always telling lots of lies,
He has a nose that's white,
He gives me a fright.

He has a yellow jumper,
And broke my dad's new bumper,
His socks are made of hay,
His shoes are grey.

If his head had a crack
His super power skin grows it back,
He lives on Mars
And likes eating cars.

**Cameron Carty  (9)**
**Our Lady & St Paul's RC Primary School**


# The Race

Quickly John raced down the track
and there was Peter at the back,
John was coming first
while Peter was slowly dying of thirst.

Huffing and puffing, Matt was coming third,
slowly followed by fourth place Bird,
as the finishing line came in sight,
the race was coming very tight,
suddenly it turned into a big fight,
to get across the finish line.

**Matthew Ashton  (9)**
**Our Lady & St Paul's RC Primary School**

# Tom, Bony Tom

Tom, bony Tom has a very hairy chest, teeth like splinters
Knickerbockers and a nose as snotty as a dump of cow's poo.
He sleeps in a sack
With an enormous toe that sticks out of his shoe.
Every day he's late for school
He's a crash of a boy and he's got really bloody fingernails
As long as the Twin Towers.
His clothes are as scruffy as a farm of hay.
He has evil red eyes and his belly is enormous.
So he can't even walk in the corridor.
He bullies all the school and he's a real troublemaker.
He makes everyone give him all their dinner money.

**Luke Campbell  (9)**
**Our Lady & St Paul's RC Primary School**


# Who Am I?

He is a rough piece of blood-red velvet,
An evil cheetah, waiting to pounce,
A dying, ugly flower desperate for everlasting life,
A hooded figure, disappearing into the distance,
A sharp blade of a killing knife,
A leaping lion, hungry for victims,
He is a blazing fire persuading people to go to him,
A vicious dog, dragging his prey to a haunted cave,
A cunning fox,
A sly snake,
He is a soul splitter.

*A: Voldemort.*

**Genevieve Easingwood  (9)**
**Our Lady & St Paul's RC Primary School**

# If I Was Queen . . .

If I was Queen . . .
I would ban every school
And put people in jail if they were being cruel,
I would live on chips
And eat toffee lips
And trap every boy in my dungeon of doom.

And with girls reunited we would start a war,
Even with nothing worth fighting for,
I would be as busy as a bee,
Earning money all for me,
My servant would be nine years old,
And very slowly going bald.

My maid would be called Matilda,
But she was shy and it nearly killed her,
And because she had rabies,
It was driving her really crazy,
So she got put in care,
With her really wild hair,
And that was the last we heard.

I would retire at 66,
Because people were making me sick,
By making a fuss,
About me being a big fat wuss,
So then I got fired,
The next day I got hired,
To be an ordinary person like you,
And that was the last you heard about me too.

**Emily McLaughlin Connell  (9)**
**Our Lady & St Paul's RC Primary School**

# Who Am I?

He is a bowling ball.
He is the biggest of them all.
He defends his country carelessly.
He is a hoover sucking up his food.
He is a stone wall.
He has a concrete belly - the biggest of them all.
He is a downside to England.
He is a lazy rebel looking for a new wife.

*A: Henry VIII.*

**Cameron Burke  (9)**
Our Lady & St Paul's RC Primary School

# Swamp Creature

He's a swamp creature,
Smell him and you will die,
He's very hungry for tea,
He's disguised in the trees,
So beware the swamp creature,
He can run very fast,
As fast as a car,
So don't go near,
He will eat you for lunch,
His head is a plum.

**Mason Cleary  (9)**
Our Lady & St Paul's RC Primary School

# My Desert Island

My desert island is in the middle of nowhere,
it has skulls, bones and even dead sharks.
It has palm trees and coconuts and at night it is dark,
spooky, quiet and terrifying as the stars dance across the sky.
The sea is like an almighty aquarium,
inside the island has rum, food and bonfire wood,
for the pirates, in a secret door on the floor.
It's an elephantine elephant.

**Danny Gregson (9)**
**Our Lady & St Paul's RC Primary School**


# Who Am I?

She's a star twinkling everlastingly from above,
A magician's talent, perfectly snatching everybody's admiration,
An almighty god of friendship, joining the world together in joy.
She's an angel floating so expertly in the beautiful sky,
A happy, chappy, old charm caring for her children,
A cheeky monkey, joking so merrily.
She's a barricade filled with love, protecting the peace of the world,
A miracle doctor, curing those who are down.

*A: Mrs O'Rourke - our headteacher.*

**Joel Stott (9)**
**Our Lady & St Paul's RC Primary School**


# Who Am I?

He is a leopard running down the wing,
He is faster than a beam of light,
He is a bulldozer knocking the ball into the net,
He is an ox in the charge,
He is a tiger tackling for victory.

*A: Cristiano Ronaldo.*

**Sam Burns (9)**
**Our Lady & St Paul's RC Primary School**

# Who Am I?

She is a glamorous, glittering piece of silk.
She is a gliding bird flying through the air.
She is a glittering diamond sparkling bright.
She is a sweet singing bird entertaining everyone.
She is a shining sun rising high above.
A light drop of rain tickling your face.

*A: Gabriella - High School Musical.*

**Toni Moores  (9)**
**Our Lady & St Paul's RC Primary School**

# Who Am I?

He is a dim green apple,
A sneaky slop,
He is a walking chubby apple,
A pain in the mud,
A brisk pants,
A lion disguised as a sweet elephant,
He is candle wax deeply plunged into his ear,
A tough weightlifter,
A travel hater.

*A: Shrek.*

**Sarah Hughes  (9)**
**Our Lady & St Paul's RC Primary School**

# Who Am I?

He's a phoenix flying into the volcano.
A cool boy saving a person's life,
Flying from the sky, going to crash.
A hero, dumber than a banana.
He's a man on fire, who can't feel it.

*A: Human torch.*

**Darnell Shaw  (9)**
**Our Lady & St Paul's RC Primary School**

# Who Am I?

He is a sporting player on a pitch.
He has an appetite for goals.
He is a festival to watch.
He is a roaring motorbike.
He is a brilliant mate.
He is an energetic person
And a strong midfielder.

*A: Nani - Manchester United.*

**James Heywood  (9)**
**Our Lady & St Paul's RC Primary School**

# Who Am I?

He is an old fashioned throne,
A heavy pig,
A worship man,
A weightlifter,
A scared chicken at night,
He is a rich pot of gold,
A bear so big.

*A: Henry VIII.*

**Danielle Davis  (9)**
**Our Lady & St Paul's RC Primary School**

# Who Am I?

She is a shining star,
A dancing queen,
A gold bracelet waiting to be worn,
She is a sparkling diamond,
A silver ring,
A lost shoe.

*A: Cinderella.*

**Georgia Langley  (10)**
**Our Lady & St Paul's RC Primary School**

# I Have A Friend

I have an alien in my wardrobe,
She loves to dress up in my clothes.
She has long silver hair and big purple eyes.
She can be a bit mean but she is always clean.
She has a big pink fluffy body.
She likes to show off her big bling bling pink diamond ring.
She has big fancy toes and loves strawberry ice cream.

**Rebecca Hilton (8)**
**Our Lady & St Paul's RC Primary School**


# Who Am I?

He is a wing of steel,
A black piece of silk,
A man who saves all,
An undercover Ferrari,
A knight in the dark,
A man stronger than a lion.

*A: Batman.*

**Jordan Yusuf (9)**
**Our Lady & St Paul's RC Primary School**


# Who Am I?

He is a fighting machine,
A bull's eye,
He is a cheetah after its prey,
A silver sword, dripping with blood
And a non-stop arrow shooter.

*A: Legolas.*

**Mark Butler (9)**
**Our Lady & St Paul's RC Primary School**

# Who Am I?

He is a super hero,
A man in bloody clothes,
A fighting mallet in a battle,
A tough cookie,
He collects mushrooms and stars to become large,
A speedy red cheetah,
A game character,
He is speedy,
He is as fast as a red fire burning the fields to dust.

*A: Super Mario from Nintendo.*

**Ryan Cosgrove  (9)**
**Our Lady & St Paul's RC Primary School**


# Who Am I?

He has a concrete right foot,
A piece of royal blue,
He is the Incredible Hulk,
He is a football master,
A cheetah searching for power,
He is a man who doesn't like losing,
He is three lions for his nation,
A champion.

*A: Frank Lampard.*

**Sam Gibson  (9)**
**Our Lady & St Paul's RC Primary School**

# Who Am I?

He is a crunching right back,
A dragon in the air,
A cheetah for speed,
A silver Audi A3 disappearing into the distance,
He is a three lion for his nation,
An alarm for strikers,
A ballerina for his sport,
A piece of sky blue,
An eager tiger, waiting to pounce up at his enemies,
A greyhound scampering down the wing,
He is a jaguar of several incredible abilities.

*A: Micah Richards.*

**Conor Sidebotham  (10)**
**Our Lady & St Paul's RC Primary School**


# Who Am I?

He has enormous goofy green ears.
An extremely popular movie star.
He is an eating machine,
But eats disgusting foods and drinks.
He brushes his teeth with bugs and slugs.
Guess who?

*A: Shrek.*

**Kevin Brews  (9)**
**Our Lady & St Paul's RC Primary School**

# Aliens From Different Planets

There is an alien in my school
He is a sneaky fool.
He lives in the toilets and no one dares to go.
He is red and has fifty five legs.
He has a wobbly nose.
He has bogeys all over his face.
He is a bit weird.
He'll jump off the Eiffel Tower head first,
                    not breaking a bone.

**Oliver Gibson  (8)**
**Our Lady & St Paul's RC Primary School**


# The Alien Who Lives Under My Bed

I have an alien, she lives under my bed,
She is always eating my mum's favourite sandwich bread,
She is really nice, but hates mice.
My alien has eyes like pies,
Her body is made of jelly and she has a big fat belly.
She went to show her mum and dad,
She can be a little bit mad.
My alien went one day, I said bye,
But she went straight away.

**Chloe Meade  (8)**
**Our Lady & St Paul's RC Primary School**

# Horse

Running so fast,
Faster than a cheetah.
Down the hill and up the hill,
Through the mill never stop running.
When you get to the stable
My auntie Mabel
Says, 'Where have you been?'
'Out with the horse,'
What do you think,
As my horse drinks
He makes a big stink.
When we ride round and round the field,
My sister watches as we go.
As my horse sleeps,
I shut the stable door and go.

**Charlotte Hampsey  (9)**
**St Bernadette's RC Primary School, Lancaster**


# Autumn

Autumn is a golden season,
The bronze leaves are falling,
The sun shines only sometimes,
But when it does, it's warming.

But autumn is rainy and cold,
I walk under crunchy leaves,
The trees are turning bare,
For it's long past bringing in the sheaves.

**Kezziah Copping  (9)**
**St Bernadette's RC Primary School, Lancaster**

# Winter

Winter
Cold dark
Snowball fights
I can see presents
Santa.

Jesus,
Joseph, Mary,
Shepherds and sheep
Three wise men, gifts
Star

Snow
Falling fast
Making snowmen
Opening the best presents
Christmas.

**Charlie Seddon (8)**
**St Bernadette's RC Primary School, Lancaster**


# I Wish It Was Winter

I wish it was winter,
Snowball fights,
Dark blue nights,
Frosty floors,
Decorated doors,
Frozen ponds,
Christmas songs,
Oh I do wish it was winter.

**Luke Stewart (9)**
**St Bernadette's RC Primary School, Lancaster**

## My Garden Swing

I sit on my garden swing
Watching the river go by.
Then my dad comes to push me
And I go very high.
I see the horses in their field
As I look over the wall.
Then my brother shouts me
And says, 'Come to the hall!'
I just ignore him and carry on swinging,
I listen hard and hear the birds singing.
I love sitting on my garden swing
Looking over the river
And listening to the birds sing.

**Laura Holden  (8)**
**St Bernadette's RC Primary School, Lancaster**


## Dancer

There was a boy
A boy who did a dance.
He stamped his feet,
He did a tap dance.
He smacked the floor
And did a wiggle.
He broke his leg,
He fell to his shoe,
He cried and cried.
I think that's enough for you.

**Alfie McPhelim  (9)**
**St Bernadette's RC Primary School, Lancaster**

# My Holidays

I love the blazing sun on my tanned face,
I love the way the rainbow colours the great blue sky,
I love licking my chocolate ice cream,
I love looking at the great blue sky,
I love to build sandcastles when the sky makes it golden
But what I love most is my . . .
Birthday!

**Chloe Ashton  (9)**
**St Bernadette's RC Primary School, Lancaster**


# Monster Munch

I know a monster red and orange,
I know a monster very hairy,
I know a monster very scary,
I know a monster who nobody has ever seen,
I know a monster who smells dreadful,
I know a monster who's my best friend,
I know a monster there is nothing he can't bend,
I know a monster who never ends.

**Morgan Townley  (8)**
**St Bernadette's RC Primary School, Lancaster**


# Scary Frights

Hallowe'en
Scary frights.
When you open the door,
Trick or treat.
Candy, we want candy.
As soon as you shut the door
Another kid is at the door
*Boom! Argh!*
Bonfire night - *bang!*
*Bang!* off they go.

**Amber Stewart  (9)**
**St Bernadette's RC Primary School, Lancaster**

# Manchester Airport

I walked into the airport, I saw the manager
Talking to the customers,
Asking what was the matter.
There were trolleys and cases
The children were running and screaming.

We passed all our tests,
We gave our passports to the lady.
She said, 'Welcome aboard.'

The plane started to run on the runway,
The air hostess came with her trolley.
'Je veux un coca?' I said.
'I'm bored,' moaned my brother.
'Mum pass me the chewing gum,' I cried.
I hate landing on the runway,
But here I am in France.

**Salma Mahmoud (9)**
**St Bernadette's RC Primary School, Lancaster**


# Spooky Hallowe'en

Spooky Hallowe'en gives everyone a fright,
Spooky Hallowe'en gives me a fright,
Spooky Hallowe'en is my favourite night,
Spooky Hallowe'en is fun when I get my chocolate bites,
So spooky Hallowe'en is coming up this night.

**Toby Jackson (10)**
**St Bernadette's RC Primary School, Lancaster**


# Winter

The colour of winter is crystal white,
The taste of winter is alright.
The smell of winter is just fine,
But altogether winter is divine.

**Eve Dodd (8)**
**St Bernadette's RC Primary School, Lancaster**

# Pets

Cats, dogs, rabbit, guinea pigs, horses, mice,
What's best for you?
Man's best friend or your *purrfect* pal?
Ride it or hide it,
Lap cats or mat cats,
Guard dogs or sit dogs,
Trained horse or untrained horse,
Mice up your jumper,
Mice in your shoe,
Which one's best for you?
Stroke 'em, groom 'em,
Coats all shiny.
Great Danes are giant,
But mice are tiny,
Get 'em in the cages,
Push 'em in the car,
Wait a few hours,
We came first in the *pet show!*

**Hannah Usher (8)**
**St Bernadette's RC Primary School, Lancaster**


# My Lovely Hamster

I love my hamster,
I adore my hamster,
I extremely love my hamster.
With a warm soft coat,
It is so ginger,
It is so white.
I could go on all night,
I absolutely love my hamster.

**Mia Eccleston (8)**
**St Bernadette's RC Primary School, Lancaster**

# Transformers In The Classroom

There are Transformers in the classroom,
Transformers everywhere.
Transformers under the tables,
Transformers on the chairs,
And if you look under the stairs,
There might be more Transformers
But
Be careful under there,
As one is good and one is bad,
Do you know which is which?

**Jamie Fowler  (8)**
**St Bernadette's RC Primary School, Lancaster**


# I Know A Monster

I know a monster blue and green,
I know a monster nobody's seen.
I know a monster with four arms,
I know a monster who lives on farms.
I know a monster who's very scary,
I know a monster who's very hairy.
I know a monster who's my friend,
I know a monster that will never end.

**Adam Buyers  (8)**
**St Bernadette's RC Primary School, Lancaster**


# Happiness

Happiness is yellow like the sand.
It smells like rocks and salt.
It feels like yellow candyfloss.
It sounds like a breeze of wind.
It tastes like grit.
It reminds me of my holiday.

**Luke Terry**
**St Mary's RC School, Accrington**

# Love

Love is red like hearts,
It smells like pie out of the oven.
It feels like a place where you feel at home.
It looks like you're about to kiss a beautiful girl.
It sounds like a lullaby when you were young.
It tastes like a warm kiss on your cheek.

**Kieran Bannan  (10)**
St Mary's RC School, Accrington


# Happiness

Happiness is pink like flowers on a bush.
It smells like a bush's flowers all together in one.
It looks like stars twinkling in the night sky.
It sounds like lives scattering in the wind.
It reminds me of good times.

**Courtney Bellas (11)**
St Mary's RC School, Accrington


# Hate

Hate is the colour orange,
Like a big bright bonfire.
It smells like bones,
My big burning bones.
It feels hot, really hot,
Like a burning piece of wood.
It looks like me dying
For hate of the bad guy.
It tastes like burns, my big sore burns.
It sounds like *sizzle, sizzle* and *bang.*
It reminds me of *death,*
The *death* of my friend.

**Liesel Baron  (10)**
St Mary's RC School, Accrington

# Fear

Fear is black because when I was younger I was scared of the dark.
It feels scary when it is dark and I don't know where I'm going.
It smells like blood pouring from the wall.
It sounds like guns shooting and axes chopping.
It tastes like blood from my jaw dripping onto my tongue.
It looks like fire, burning through my skin.
It reminds me of the way my uncle died.

**Lewis Noone & Nicholas Widdop  (10)**
**St Mary's RC School, Accrington**

# Sadness

Sadness is black, like moping faces of people at a cremation.
It smells like the smell of disinfectant at a hospital.
It reminds me of my deceased grandparents.
It looks like a crying urchin.
It tastes like raw egg.
It feels like a ripped up heart.
It sounds like low bass music.

**Jack Taylor  (10)**
**St Mary's RC School, Accrington**

# Happiness

Happiness is turquoise like the sea.
It smells like newly cut grass.
It feels like when I put on a football shirt.
It looks like a football.
It tastes like cinnamon.
It sounds like an MP3 player.
It reminds me of my holiday.

**Joseph Dwyer  (10)**
**St Mary's RC School, Accrington**

# Happiness

Happiness is blue, like the sea from my hols.
It smells like salt.
It tastes like chocolate.
It looks like yellow sand.
It sounds like waves clashing together.
It reminds me of the Isle of Wight.

**Joshua Haworth  (11)**
**St Mary's RC School, Accrington**

# Fear

Fear is black like the dark night.
It smells like smoke, like a vampire.
It feels like fingers on the back of a neck.
It looks like great beady, bloodshot stone eyes.
It tastes like dry bitter spit and blood.
It sounds like your heart beating out of rate.
It feels like you're alone and something is creeping in the dark
and is going to get you.
It reminds me of everything I fear like ghosts and monsters.
That is fear.

**James Kelly  (10)**
**St Mary's RC School, Accrington**

# My Poem

Happiness is green, like playing football,
It smells like dinner's just been laid out on the table.
It feels like my cat.
It looks like my mum and dad's enormous family tree.
It tastes like a massive chocolate factory.
It sounds like Liverpool have just scored to make it a big victory.
It reminds me of my best friends.

**Dominic Jack Lord  (10)**
**St Mary's RC School, Accrington**

# Happiness

Happiness is green like the Christmas tree at Christmas.
It smells like Christmas dinner when I come down into the kitchen.
It feels like I am a giddy five-year-old again, when I open
my presents.
It looks like decorations at a town festival.
It sounds like jingle bells everywhere.
It tastes like nice yummy turkey.
It reminds me of my family together.

**Dominic Meadowcroft  (11)**
**St Mary's RC School, Accrington**


# Happiness

Happiness is red like my favourite colour.
It smells of Lynx Vice.
It feels like a soft duvet.
It looks like the beautiful sunset.
It sounds like cheering when I score.
It reminds me of my brilliant holiday in Scotland.
It tastes of chocolate.

**Matthew Alan Lord  (10)**
**St Mary's RC School, Accrington**


# Hate

Hate is dark blue like the stormy seas.
It smells like burnt wood.
It reminds me of war, hostility between countries.
It looks like a storm.
It tastes like decomposing muscle.
It feels like your stomach being torn out.
It sounds like an atom bomb exploding.

**Daniel Robinson  (10)**
**St Mary's RC School, Accrington**

# Happiness

Happiness is green like a football pitch,
It smells like Lynx Vice,
It tastes like hot melted chocolate,
It feels like a soft duvet,
It looks like the sunset,
It sounds like tearing of paper on Christmas Day,
It reminds me of winning a football tournament.

**Connor Taylor  (10)**
**St Mary's RC School, Accrington**


# Sadness

Sadness is colourless like teardrops from my eyes.
It smells like my dad's cooking.
It tastes like an onion.
It looks like people who are ill.
It sounds like opera music.
It reminds me of a funeral.

**Hannah Young  (10)**
**St Mary's RC School, Accrington**


# Anger

The colour of anger is dark red, and people like my brother
                                who get me angry.
Anger smells like twigs and leaves burning.
Anger makes me feel like swinging for someone.

**Tyler Chapman**
**St Mary's RC School, Accrington**

# Emotions Of Hate

Hate is red like the centre of a dartboard.
Hate smells like cigarettes.
Hate feels like losing to a rival.
Hate tastes like mashed potato.
Hate looks like someone who has hurt you.
Hate reminds me of losing on the last level of a PS2 game.

**Blaise Dewar  (10)**
**St Mary's RC School, Accrington**

# Happiness

Happiness looks like people jumping around.
Happiness feels like Man United winning.
Happiness sounds like tearing open the presents
                             on Christmas morning.
Happiness smells like melted chocolate.
Happiness will be when I get a Porsche 911 GTR.

**Jamie Gardner  (10)**
**St Mary's RC School, Accrington**

# Happiness

Happiness is green, new-mown grass.
It smells like pollen, the flowers start to grow.
It feels like waves splashing on my face.
It looks like a big fluffy bunny.
It tastes like strawberries nice and sweet.
It reminds me of days at the beach and park.
It sounds like music dancing in the air.

**Holly Moore  (10)**
**St Mary's RC School, Accrington**

# Hate

Hate is red like the Devil.
Hate smells smoky like fire and burning twigs.
Hate feels like losing to an enemy.
Hate looks like blood and being hurt.
Hate reminds me of falling out with my friends.
Hate sounds like lots of people arguing.
Hate makes me feel angry.

**Ryan Ormerod (10)**
**St Mary's RC School, Accrington**


# Love

Love is red like a rose.
Love smells like lovely flowers.
It tastes like strawberries.
It sounds like gentle flowing water.
Love is happiness.
It feels like a soft cushion.
Love reminds me of nice things.

**Shannon Norris (10)**
**St Mary's RC School, Accrington**


# Happiness

Happiness is yellow like the sun.
It smells like roses.
It feels like my sister.
It looks like a newborn baby.
It sounds like the sea.
It reminds me of my holidays.

**Sophie Remez**
**St Mary's RC School, Accrington**

# The Magic Box

*(Based on 'Magic Box' by Kit Wright)*

I will put in my box . . .

The first ruby-red berry of autumn.
The first sweet smelling rose to bloom.
The gentle ponies trotting along the country lane.

I will put in my box . . .

The nasty nip of a crab as I stand on its smooth shell.
The sudden pain of a lobster biting me as its anger heats up.
A rapid *roar* of a T-rex as it protects its young.

I will put in my box . . .

A cute rabbit with a fluffy white tail.
The glimpse of a shy little dormouse
And the touch of my dog's furry hair.

I will put in my box . . .

A time machine painted in roses.
The sound of bombs hitting the ground in World War II.
An angry caveman hitting me on the head.

My box is made out of . . .

Magic jewels,
Precious stones,
Deadly sharks' teeth.

My box is used for
Saving cute cuddly animals that get deadly diseases.

**Harriet Lodge  (10)**
**Sabden Primary School**

# The Magic Box

*(Based on 'Magic Box' by Kit Wright)*

I will put into my box . . .

Shiny fish jumping out of the sea.
A goldfish leaping out of its glass bowl.
The shiny silk of a tiger's fur.

I will put in my box . . .

Ruby-red apples dangling on the trees.
The smell of sausage and egg on a sunny morning.
The taste of my grandma's homemade apple pie.

I will put in my box . . .

The swish of colour pompoms.
The sparkle of the pretty fireworks in the sky.
A witch whizzing over Pendle Hill.

My box is made from . . .

Sparkling jewels like rubies, emeralds and sapphires
From the Queen's crown.

I am going to use it for . . .

Putting all my special memories in.

**Kyra Mellows  (9)**
**Sabden Primary School**

# The Magic Box

*(Based on 'Magic Box' by Kit Wright)*

I will put into my box . . .

The sound of a lion sleeping in the jungle.
The salty tears that run down your cheeks.
The soft and silky touch of a ruby-red rose petal.

I will put into my box . . .

Gentle whispers from those who are long forgotten.
Sweet smells of freshly baked brown bread.
The cold and windy breeze on your face.

I will put into my box . . .

Glimmering shines of a thousand sparkling diamonds.
Cries of a small child when she has fallen.
The pitter-patter of raindrops.

My box is fashioned from ice corners, with rims of gold.
The lid is covered with dazzling hearts, with pearl centres.
The sides are decorated with the softest fur in the world.

**Elena Haythornthwaite  (9)**
**Sabden Primary School**

# The Magic Box

*(Based on 'Magic Box' by Kit Wright)*

I will put into my box . . .

The sprinkled frost on the window on an autumn morning.
A fresh layer of sparkling snow on your drive.
Sharp nipping air on Christmas Day.

I will put into my box . . .

The crackle of a ruby-red fire flickering on the wood.
The crispy gold roast potato on a Sunday night.
The scent of a mouth-watering warm chocolate cake.

I will put into my box . . .

The cheerful laughter of a toddler when she has achieved a step.
A smooth white pearl nestled inside a purple clam, sparkling in
                                        the beam of the sun.
The warmth of the paper wrapping up those delicious hot chips.
The rough tongue of a dog in the morning.

My box is made out of . . .

The largest ruby from the deepest mine.
The shiniest gold from a dragon's cave.
A huge silver padlock that glows in the moonlight.
Sprinkled fairy dust, a rainbow of colours.

**Eleanor White  (10)**
**Sabden Primary School**

# The Magic Box

*(Based on 'Magic Box' by Kit Wright)*

I will put into my box . . .

A fruity creamy ice cream melting on the surface of the spoon.
A lick of the finest chocolate, coated in dripping hot caramel.
Lemon cake, steaming straight from the hot oven.

I will put into my box . . .

An owl hooting at the dead of night.
A ghost swirling up and down the broken-down mansion as it creaks.
The glistening white moon in the distant sky.

I will put into my box . . .

Bolting flames raging out of the black dead volcano.
A fire sounding like tin foil as it sparkles in the sun.
The shimmering first blush of spring.

My box is fashioned from ice and diamonds and the ten best
                                        stars in the Universe.
With lipstick and make-up in the centre of the lid.
I will look after my box forever.

**Ruby Willett  (9)**
**Sabden Primary School**

# The Magic Box

*(Based on 'Magic Box' by Kit Wright)*

I will put into my box . . .

The bang of an exploding firework, bursting into light.
The flame of the first Bonfire Night.
The fizz of a sparkler being waved about.

I will put into my box . . .

The fur of the tiger, the very last one.
The cry of the great white shark.
The *roar* of a golden lion, hunting in the night.

I will put into my box . . .

The taste of melting chocolate, poured into a cup.
The smell of tender golden sausages sizzling in a pan.
The sight of thick crispy Christmas pudding, the cherry still on top.

I will put into my box . . .

The sparkle of diamonds stuck in a coastal wet cave.
The sea glistening, crashing against the slippery rocks.
The grainy sand washing away as the sea laps over it.

I will put into my box . . .

The wail of a banshee from beyond the grave.
The shake of bones from the skeleton's hand.
The caw of a crow soaring high above.

My box is fashioned with eagle feathers,
The snow from Mount Everest and the lock is gold,
The key is silver.

I will open my box when I need to.

**Emily Greenhalgh (9)**
**Sabden Primary School**

# The Magic Box

*(Based on 'Magic Box' by Kit Wright)*

I will put into my box . . .

The blood of a witch's coal-black cat,
The matted hair of an old Chinese dragon,
A golden eagle's heart, huge and still beating.

I will put into my box . . .

The first cry of a newborn baby,
The swish of an osprey's giant wing,
The ghostly spirits on a grey foggy night.

I will put into my box . . .

The rough tongue sliced from a tiger,
The view of a lifetime climbing Ben Nevis,
The smell of salty waters from the Atlantic.

My box is fashioned from light, air and steel,
With moons on the lid and secrets in the corners.
Its hinges are the joints of tiny house martins.

I shall kneel in my box,
And pray to the gods,
To calm me down when I'm angry.

**Rhiannon Wickham (9)**
**Sabden Primary School**

# The Magic Box

*(Based on 'Magic Box' by Kit Wright)*

In my box I will put . . .

The whisper of my friend telling me all her secrets.
All the purrs and miaows of my cat at night wanting her food.
The noise of my auntie rocking the new baby to sleep.

In my box I will put . . .

Chocolate drizzling down a fountain endlessly, straight
into my mouth.
Cheesecake with cream and strawberries poured on top.
Birthday cake being cut and almost ready to eat.

In my box I will put . . .

A shooting star that was caught from the sky last night.
Golden Greek coins found deep in the Atlantic Ocean.
The biggest free roller coaster in the whole world.
A magical snowman that will never melt.

My box will be made of . . .

The finest silk made in Japan and sent to England specially.
A secret lock that only opens when I tell it to.
The sides are made out of real silver and need polishing every
day to keep it extra shiny.

My box will be used for . . .

Keeping every little memory from my life, so when I am older
I can look at them.

**Jaeger Bywater  (10)**
**Sabden Primary School**

# The Magic Box

*(Based on 'Magic Box' by Kit Wright)*

I will put into my box . . .

The crackle of popcorn in the pan.
The spitting of an egg in the sizzler.
The crunch of crisps when I put them into my mouth.

I will put into my box . . .

The gentle gnawing of my hamster nibbling his cage.
The sound of a horse galloping on the rustling leaves.
The shiny red sparkle of my hamster's eyes.

I will put into my box . . .

The sight of Liverpool winning every cup.
The swish of pompoms when Man Utd win every match.
One cold drop of water from an Arctic iceberg.

I will put into my box . . .

The boom of the best music in the world.
The glisten of the first star that comes out.
The sparkle of my very own birthstone.

My box is fashioned with the biggest emerald in the world
And the rings of wedding bells.

I will use my box for keeping secrets
And they will never come out.

**Bethany Ashton  (9)**
**Sabden Primary School**

# The Magic Box

*(Based on 'Magic Box' by Kit Wright)*

I will put in my magic box . . .

A diamond as big as a mountain.
The sound of a 100 coins clattering on the golden floor.
A month-old dolphin gliding through the water.
The soft wool of the newborn lamb.

I will put in my magic box . . .

The wand of the garden.
The sand of rose petals.
The damp smell of a rainforest.

I will put in my magic box . . .

Manchester United winning every World Cup.
The taste of freshly baked chocolate cake.

My box is made from wood
And precious stones.

**Shane Hollinrake  (9)**
**Sabden Primary School**


# The Raindrop

A shiny raindrop is like an apple falling off a tree,
Or a grenade blowing up,
Like a tennis ball gliding through the air,
Or an apple next to a branch.
The raindrop drips like a broken tap
Or a shiny moon or a bright blue balloon.
It has a colourful rainbow trapped inside.

**Robert Hodge  (9)**
**Trinity & St Michael's CE School**

# The Senses Of Me

Such a sight I saw:
Trees rocking in the wind with their leaves
Rustling and fluttering down like butterflies.
It made me feel frosty and shivery.
Such a sight.

Such a sound I heard:
A little baby bird chirping in its warm cosy nest,
On a wintry damp morning.
It sounded happy and peaceful.
Such a sound I heard.

Such food I tasted:
A pink chewy jelly baby in my mouth,
It was tasty and scrumptious.
It made me feel cheerful and delighted.
Such food I tasted.

Such a smell I smelt:
A chocolate fountain trickling with delight, oozing and hot.
It was like lava running down a volcano.
It made me feel hungry and warm.
Such food I tasted.

Such soft fur I felt:
A puppy's silky coat
It was warm and cosy.
It made me feel dozy and cuddly.
Such soft fur I felt.

**Megan Squire  (10)**
**Trinity & St Michael's CE School**

# The Raindrop

The raindrop is like a penny spinning on a glowing kitchen floor,
Or an eye glaring at a marvellous, crimson and amber sparkling
firework show.
Like a spangley star shining as other children play,
Or a full stop at the end of a sentence making a reader come
to an end.
The raindrop trickles like a tasty melting chocolate bar,
Or a watery eye,
Or a disgusting tablespoon of medicine spilling off the silver spoon.
It has colourful water clashing all around it.

**Jessica Carroll  (9)**
**Trinity & St Michael's CE School**


# The Raindrop

The raindrop is like a shimmering apple, sparkling in
the midnight moonlight,
Or a letter O,
Or an eye popping out of somebody's head.
Like a Christmas pudding being chopped in half,
Or a bullet point bulging.
The raindrop is like a melting chocolate bar,
Or a piece of coal in a fire,
Or a hole that a rabbit has burrowed.
It's like water splashing around.

**Charlotte Emily Newton  (9)**
**Trinity & St Michael's CE School**

# The Raindrop

The encircled raindrop is like a perfectly pink planet
Hurtling down to a soggy Earth,
Or a well burnished cannonball.
Like a shimmering, super blue moon glimmering in the dusky night
Or a sky-blue eye blinking because of the gleaming sun.
The raindrop glitters like a disco ball
Shimmering in the coloured lights on the oak floor,
Or a brand new ring shining from the light of a diamond
Or a shooting star in the dark midnight sky.
It has the world trapped inside its wobbly walls of water,
towering high.

**Ross Watson  (9)**
**Trinity & St Michael's CE School**


# The Raindrop

The beautiful raindrop
Breaks into pieces as it hits the ground
Like a glass jar smashing
Or a venomous snake's touch
Or a shiny orange on a branch
Like a carefully carved cannonball
From a metal workshop.
The raindrop dribbles like a runny nose
Or a slimy green thing,
Or a light-noted ping.
It has blinding light trapped inside.

**Daniel Clarke  (10)**
**Trinity & St Michael's CE School**

# The Senses Of The World

Such a sight I saw:
A cloud skimming across the sky,
It was soaring like the wind in the gleaming sun.
It made me feel special and peaceful.
Such a sight I saw.

Such a sound I heard:
A collection of glistening water lashing against the rocks of
the waterfall.
The streaming silky water was like a silver river of light.
It made me feel like a glowing angel.
Such a sound I heard.

Such a smell I smelt:
A scarlet rose standing out from the rest of the flower bed.
It smelt fresh and fragrant like my mum's favourite perfume.
It made me feel happy and joyful like a spring lamb leaping
and bouncing amongst the daffodils.
Such a smell I smelt.

Such soft wool I felt:
A warm sheepskin rug in front of the burning flames of the fireplace.
It was like a winter's day in your snuggest jumper.
It made me feel dozy and sleepy like a shepherd watching his flock.
Such soft wool I felt.

Such food I tasted:
A smooth chocolate fondue with sweet strawberries
and marshmallows.
It was a chocolate heaven in its own special way, with
strawberry trees.
It made me feel that I wished everything was chocolate.
Such food I tasted.

**Annie Williams  (9)**
**Trinity & St Michael's CE School**

# Such A . . .

Such a sight I saw:
Clouds flowing by in the midnight sky.
They were like fluffy marshmallows just about to be dropped
Into a mug of hot chocolate.
They were cradling me in their arms.
Such a sight I saw.

Such a sound I heard:
A magnificent jumbo jet's engine,
Rumbling and tumbling in my head.
I felt excited at its rage.
Such a sound I heard.

Such a smell I smelt:
The smell of cheesy pizza with pepperoni on top,
A hot cake of bread with a juicy layer of tomato.
It made me have bubbles in my tummy.
Such a smell I smelt.

Such a good feeling I felt:
Cold snow on my nose.
It was like fluffy white cotton wool pads.
I was chilly but warm inside, it was fuzzy and fun.
Such a good feeling I felt.

Such good food I tasted:
Chocolate that was mouth-watering in my slobbering mouth
Fluffy and warm when it ran down my throat.
I felt bubbly and full of fun.
Such good food I tasted.

**Ashley Singleton  (10)**
**Trinity & St Michael's CE School**

# Such A Sense

Such a taste:
A dark brown, warm crispy duck on a smooth pancake,
It was carefully placed into my eager mouth.
It made me feel like hungry King Henry VIII.
Such a taste.

Such a smell:
Multicoloured petrol lying in the bright sun.
It was like all kinds of food colourings spilt into a glass of water.
It made me feel sleepy and dozy.
Such a smell.

Such a sound:
A squealing pig eating some greasy bacon.
It was like an old man snoring.
It made me feel piggish and baby-like.
Such a sound.

Such a feeling:
The shiny paintwork on a Lamborghini hidden in a dark garage.
Its warm engine was like a dying fire.
It made me feel rich and fast.
Such a feeling.

Such a sight:
A bloody butcher's store,
Like an open wound covered in maggots and leeches
In the humid rainforest.
It made me feel horribly sick.

**Robbie Scott  (10)**
**Trinity & St Michael's CE School**

# The Five Senses

Such a sight I saw:
A piece of beef cooking in the oven, steaming and flat,
It was moving in the pan like a wobbly jelly,
It made me feel like eating and drinking.
Such a sight I saw.

Such a sound I heard:
A brass band playing in the street,
It sounded like a brass band that had been practising every day,
It made me feel like dancing.
Such a sound I heard.

Such a smell I smelled:
A can of tomato soup boiling in a pan,
It was like smelling a can of tomatoes,
It made me feel like having a can of it myself.
Such a smell I smelled.

Such a taste I tasted:
A bag of chips from Croston Chippy,
It was like eating the best chips in the world,
It made me feel like coming back every day.
Such a taste I tasted.

Such a touch I touched:
A long black cat sitting on a long black wall,
It was like feeling a hot water bottle cover.
It made me feel like buying a cat myself.
Such a touch I touched.

**Isobel Lockwood  (9)**
**Trinity & St Michael's CE School**

# Such A Sound

Such a sound:
The dog barking in the street,
It reminds me of a bird soaring through the dim winter light,
It makes me feel like I'm invincible.
Such a sound.

Such a smell:
The running chocolate fountain in the sweet shop window,
It reminds me of a load of people dancing around an African fire.
It makes me feel warm, cosy and right at home.
Such a smell.

Such a taste:
The melting chocolate ice cream on my tongue.
It makes me feel hot and cold at the same time.
Such a taste.

**Amelia Rose Turner (9)**
**Trinity & St Michael's CE School**


# The Raindrop

The glistening raindrop is like a colourful disco ball,
Or a rugby ball.
Like a crazy crackling Rice Krispie,
Or a pimple on a face.
The raindrop shimmers like the moon,
Or a balloon,
Or a silver spoon.
It has sparkling spring water in it.

**Joe Wickstead (9)**
**Trinity & St Michael's CE School**

# Five Senses

Such a taste:
It's like a chocolate fountain running down my neck,
It's like chocolate spread on warm toast.
It makes me feel excited.
Such a taste.

Such a sight:
It's like a car going straight past me at 100mph,
It's like a bird flying gently through the rustling leaves of a tree.
It makes me feel cool.
Such a sight.

Such a smell:
It's like a bomb blowing up a mile away,
It's a can of diesel.
It makes me feel cool.
Such a sight.

Such a touch:
It's like being famous,
It's the World Cup football under my feet.
It makes me feel joyful.
Such a touch.

Such a sound:
It's a nice smooth sound,
It's birds singing.
It makes me feel happy.
Such a sound.

**Jack Cairns (9)**
**Trinity & St Michael's CE School**

# The Raindrop

The raindrop is like a soft orange hanging from a wooden branch,
Or a cannonball smashing into a fort -
Like a gigantic wart on the end of a bent nose,
Or a black full stop hovering at the end of a page.
The raindrop drips like an icicle melting with the sun inside it,
Or a big white moon,
Or a shiny teaspoon.
The raindrop has air bubbles inside
Bursting like fireworks in November.

**Jack Marsh (10)**
**Trinity & St Michael's CE School**


# The Raindrop

The raindrop sits small and shy,
Like a star shining brightly in a midnight sky,
Or a beautiful bubble of light -
Or a planet in the pitch-black night.
Like a fox's beady eye from his cunning face,
Or a glossy badge for the winner of the race.
The raindrop stands out like a whisper with a shout,
Or a big red button on a radio playing loud,
Or the face of a rich king in a poor crowd.
It has the light of the sky shining through it.

**Abby Joanna Tomlinson (9)**
**Trinity & St Michael's CE School**

# The Raindrop

The clear round raindrop is like a bowling ball curling down the alley.
Or a cricket ball -
Or a lumpy wart on a face,
Like a blue bomb exploding from the eye of a cannon,
Or a bright blue egg.
The raindrop drips like melting chocolate on a cake,
Or slime dripping out of the walls in a haunted house,
Or a snowball melting in the sun.
It has a mysterious see-through effect trapped inside
                                        made of millions of bubbles.

**Louis Jordan  (9)**
**Trinity & St Michael's CE School**


# The Raindrop

The raindrop is like a beaming full moon rising at dawn,
Or a baked bean perched on a plate -
Like a pie steaming and sizzling
Or a pimple between an eye and a nose pumping up and down.
The raindrop is like a spinning disco ball glittering,
Shining in the moonlight,
Or an orbiting, shining blue moon,
Or a whizzing, popping party balloon.
It has a football dribbling inside
Scoring a goal, what a success!

**Emily Caunce  (10)**
**Trinity & St Michael's CE School**

# The Raindrop

The wet raindrop is like a light brown freckle on an oval red-hot face,
Or a bull's-eye on a profession dartboard -
Like a bouncing ball bounding everywhere
Or a shiny red apple peeping through some leaves.
The raindrop drips like a slimy, runny nose
Or a shooting star flying across the midnight sky,
Or a melting iceberg from the North Pole.
It has a magic world inside.

**Liam Buckley (9)**
**Trinity & St Michael's CE School**


# The Raindrop

The raindrop is like the spinning planet Earth of the solar system,
Or a huge traffic light -
Like a huge basketball from a basketball court,
Or a small palm of a hand between five ferocious, huge fingers.
The raindrop whizzes around like a shooting star,
Or the top of a letter P,
Or the bottom of a letter B.

**Nathan Stott (9)**
**Trinity & St Michael's CE School**


# The Raindrop

The glimmering raindrop glowed like a bubble in the sky,
Or a glamorous crystal ball -
Like a crazy, crackling cauldron bubbling from the witch's cave,
Or a clear bubble bouncing in the air.
The raindrop is like a delicious melting chocolate bar,
Or a big bright moon,
Or a big fat balloon.
It has clear lights and torrents of water
            dropping down into the sea.

**Robert Bretherton (9)**
**Trinity & St Michael's CE School**

# The Raindrop

The raindrop is like a glowing apple on a blossom tree,
Or a beaming diamond.

Like a lake shining and swiftly rippling,
Or a sky-blue eye blinking in the summer sky.

Like a melting icicle hanging from the guttering,
Or a melting snowflake fading on the grass,

Or a bursting balloon with water inside it -
A raindrop.

**Matthew Wignall  (10)**
**Trinity & St Michael's CE School**


# The Raindrop

The bright raindrop is like a gleaming eyeball,
Or a shiny snowball.
Like a blue football whizzing through the air,
Or a shiny apple between two trees.
The raindrop is like drizzling blood,
Or a pork pie,
Or a dead fly.

**Chaise Richards  (9)**
**Trinity & St Michael's CE School**


# The Raindrop

The raindrop is like black pepper grinding out of its mill,
Or a rusty doorknob,
Or a scorching pie between two pasties.
Like a shiny stinger on the back of someone's leg.
The raindrop is like a slippery football between the goalie's hands,
Or a muddy footprint filling up with water.
Like a piping hot pie,
A real football treat, eaten in the bright blue sky!

**Declan Roy Stewart  (9)**
**Trinity & St Michael's CE School**

# The Raindrop

The shiny raindrop speckled on the floor
Like a shiny eye
Or a crystal ball.
Like a shiny apple.
The raindrop is like two bubbles
Bouncing like sparkling stars
Or sparkling crystal.
It has the sun trapped inside.

**Benjamin Bickerstaffe (9)**
Trinity & St Michael's CE School


# The Raindrop

The soggy raindrop is like a soaring football
Or a full moon.
Like a petite planet plunging,
Or a full stop rolling off a page.
The raindrops shines like a piece of marble,
Or a shimmering moon,
Or a 40th birthday balloon.
It has crystals of many colours trapped inside.

**Bethany Cairns (9)**
Trinity & St Michael's CE School


# The Raindrop

The raindrop is weak like a toddler bird's beak,
Or a bouncy blue ball in a shop -
The raindrop is like a popping balloon,
Like a blue sky or a big pie in the sky.
It has the water inside reflecting colours.

**James Kenneth Wignall (10)**
Trinity & St Michael's CE School

# Young Writers Information

We hope you have enjoyed reading this book - and that you will continue to enjoy it in the coming years.

If you like reading and writing poetry drop us a line, or give us a call, and we'll send you a free information pack.

Alternatively if you would like to order further copies of this book or any of our other titles, then please give us a call or log onto our website at www.youngwriters.co.uk

**Young Writers Information**
**Remus House**
**Coltsfoot Drive**
**Peterborough**
**PE2 9JX**

**(01733) 890066**